D0596671

STAR GUIDE
TO GUYS

THIS BOOK WITHDRAWN FROM
THE RECORDS OF THE
MID-CONTINENT PUBLIC LIBRARY

OCT 0 5

133.5864677 P419
Perkins, Elizabeth.
Star guide to guys

MID-CONTINENT PUBLIC LIBRARY
Claycomo Branch
309 N.E. 69 Highway
Claycomo, MO 64119

CL

About the Author

Elizabeth Perkins is a writer and businesswoman in the Southwest. She is the author of *When Venus Collides with Mars: A Woman's Guide to Why Men Act the Way They Do*, and her articles have appeared in *Bowler's Journal, Dell Horoscope, Golf for Women*, and *American Astrology*. Beginning in 1998, she created and maintained an award-winning website, and produced a monthly internet astrology newsletter for women for several years. She recently launched a new website:

www.astrologywithelizabeth.com

To Write to the Author

If you wish to contact the author or would like more information about this book, please write to the author in care of Llewellyn Worldwide and we will forward your request. Both the author and publisher appreciate hearing from you and learning of your enjoyment of this book and how it has helped you. Llewellyn Worldwide cannot guarantee that every letter written to the author can be answered, but all will be forwarded. Please write to:

Elizabeth Perkins
℅ Llewellyn Worldwide
2143 Wooddale Drive, Dept.0-7387-0954-9
Woodbury, Minnesota 55125-2989, U.S.A.
Please enclose a self-addressed stamped envelope for reply,
or $1.00 to cover costs. If outside the U.S.A., enclose
international postal reply coupon.

Many of Llewellyn's authors have websites with additional information and resources. For more information, please visit our website at http://www.llewellyn.com.

☆ ☆ ☆ ☆ ☆ ☆ ☆ ☆ ☆ ☆ ☆ ☆ ☆ ☆ ☆ ☆ ☆

STAR GUIDE
TO ⊙ GUYS

☆ ☆ ☆ ☆ ☆ ☆ ☆ ☆ ☆ ☆ ☆ ☆ ☆ ☆ ☆ ☆ ☆

How to Live Happily With Him . . .

or Without Him

Elizabeth Perkins

Llewellyn Publications
Woodbury, Minnesota

MID-CONTINENT PUBLIC LIBRARY
Claycomo Branch
309 N.E. 69 Highway
Claycomo, MO 64119

CL

MID-CONTINENT PUBLIC LIBRARY

3 0000 12842047 2

Star Guide to Guys: How to Live Happily With Him . . . or Without Him © 2007 by Elizabeth Perkins. All rights reserved. No part of this book may be used or reproduced in any manner whatsoever, including Internet usage, without written permission from Llewellyn Publications except in the case of brief quotations embodied in critical articles and reviews.

First Edition
First Printing, 2007

Cover art © Photographer: George Doyle/Stockbyte Platinum/Getty Images
Cover design by Lisa Novak
Editing by Connie Hill
Llewellyn is a registered trademark of Llewellyn Worldwide, Ltd.

Cover model(s) used for illustrative purposes only, and may not endorse or represent the book's subject.

Library of Congress Cataloging-in-Publication Data
Perkins, Elizabeth.
  Star guide to guys : how to live happily with him—or without him / Elizabeth Perkins.
      p. cm.
  ISBN 13: 978-0-7387-0954-3
  ISBN 10: 0-7387-0954-9
    1. Astrology.   2. Women—Psychology—Miscellanea.   3. Man-woman relationships—Miscellanea.   I. Title.

BF1729.W64P47   2007
133.5'864677—dc22   2006048738

Llewellyn Worldwide does not participate in, endorse, or have any authority or responsibility concerning private business transactions between our authors and the public.
  All mail addressed to the author is forwarded but the publisher cannot, unless specifically instructed by the author, give out an address or phone number.
  Any Internet references contained in this work are current at publication time, but the publisher cannot guarantee that a specific location will continue to be maintained. Please refer to the publisher's website for links to authors' websites and other sources.

Llewellyn Publications
A Division of Llewellyn Worldwide, Ltd.
2143 Wooddale Drive, Dept. 0-7387-0954-9
Woodbury, Minnesota 55125-2989, U.S.A.
www.llewellyn.com

Printed in the United States of America

Dedication

To all women, with the hope that we can be as gentle and generous to ourselves as we are to others.

And to my ex-husbands and ex-lovers: Thank you for the lessons you taught me, the experiences that strengthened me and, most of all, for the knowledge that the biggest love of all—self-love—is where it all begins.

E. P.

Contents

Part Three: On Your Own

How to be happy with him . . . or without him.
Look to your Sun sign for your greatest strengths

Introduction

Women's rule of thumb:
If it has tires or testicles, you're going to have trouble with it.
—Sign in women's restroom at Dick's Resort, Dallas, Texas

Why are men so clueless? Take the case of Ed and Melissa Turner (not their real names), the parents of four active young boys. Life was proceeding at its usual hectic but normal pace until Melissa began having blackouts. She was frightened, but extensive tests found nothing physically wrong. The doctor told Melissa her blackouts were caused by stress. His advice? Find ways to lessen the stress and/or learn how to cope with it.

Melissa began to think of how they might simplify things so their lives would be less chaotic. She knew it wouldn't be easy and she was prepared for that. What she wasn't prepared for was her husband's response: he brought home a Golden Retriever puppy! Obviously, he believed a puppy would be the perfect cheerer-upper. When Melissa told her girlfriends about it, they laughed and nodded in sympathy. (By the way, they found a good home for the dog.)

As much as we try to educate men, they can still be clueless about things *we* think should be obvious. This much we know: men and women speak different languages and have different approaches to life. This holds true in astrology as well; a female Capricorn won't have exactly the same traits as a male Capricorn.

Perhaps Ed Turner wasn't clueless as much as on a different wavelength. Bringing home a puppy sounds like an idea hatched by an impetuous Aries. If Melissa was familiar with his Sun sign, she might have seen his gift for what it was—a sincere effort to help by an impulsive Aries—and not just a thoughtless act by an insensitive husband. When we use astrology to give us insight into personality, we are that much further ahead in understanding ourselves . . . and men.

Can you live with him . . . should you try?

All too often, we women get emotionally involved with a man before we know what we're getting into. It's possible to save yourself a lot of trouble and heartbreak by checking out a man's astrological chart *before* you get to your emotional point of no return.

By reading up on his Sun sign in Part One, you'll learn about his negative traits, his good ones, his likes and dislikes, and, in general, what makes him tick. Do his goals, desires, and personality complement yours or will they cause friction? At the end of each male Sun sign description are the "Dos and Don'ts" for living with that sign.

Find out more about you

Just as important as learning about him is learning about *your* relationship needs and personality style. In Part Two, you can do just that. When you are aware of your most important issues, you can determine if he's a great guy *for you,* or just a great guy. Then look up any of the signs and see how it goes with yours—just what you always wanted to know!

For the single woman

All women will spend part of their lives without a partner—that's a given. With the high divorce rate and the way we outlive men, it could be a big part. Do you know what your strengths and assets are when it comes to being happy as a single woman? In Part Three, you can look up your Sun sign and learn how it copes with being alone, and where it excels. I hope it helps you in your approach to the single life, even if it's merely an episode between relationships.

We all have the power to be happy, whether we have a man in our life or not. When we enjoy loving relationships with others, pursue our interests, and love ourselves enough to see that our needs are met—life can be sweet, no matter what.

☆ ☆ ☆ ☆ ☆ ☆ ☆ ☆ ☆ ☆ ☆ ☆ ☆ ☆ ☆ ☆

Part One: All About Him

Everything you need to know about the twelve signs in men

(plus Dos and Don'ts for each sign)

☆ ☆ ☆ ☆ ☆ ☆ ☆ ☆ ☆ ☆ ☆ ☆ ☆ ☆ ☆ ☆

PROLOGUE

ABOUT SUN SIGNS

There's no such thing as a 100 percent Aries or a 100 percent *anything* because no one has all ten planets in one sign. However, knowing a person's Sun sign gives us a lot of information we wouldn't otherwise have, and is a good indication of personality. A rule of thumb is that the following descriptions will have an accuracy range of 70 to 90 percent.

People are complicated . . . and so is astrology. To get a precise picture of an individual, a chart must be erected using the date, time, and place of birth. You can do that with a professional astrologer, or go online to order a chart interpretation, sometimes called a "natal chart" or "personality profile." You will be amazed at the accuracy. Many psychologists use astrology as a shortcut to help them understand their clients and shorten the duration of therapy.

After the Sun sign, the next in importance are the Moon and Ascendant, or Rising sign. If you know a man's Moon or Ascendant, read those paragraphs as well for more information. The following list will help you determine his Sun sign.

If he was born between:	his Sun sign is:
March 21–April 19	Aries
April 20–May 20	Taurus
May 21–June 21	Gemini
June 22–July 22	Cancer

July 23–August 22	Leo
August 23–September 22	Virgo
September 23–October 22	Libra
October 23–November 21	Scorpio
November 22–December 21	Sagittarius
December 22–January 19	Capricorn
January 20–February 18	Aquarius
February 19–March 20	Pisces

About the dates: From year to year, the dates when new signs begin can change by a day or two. If a birthday falls within one or two days of a sign change, a computer chart can determine the exact Sun sign.

Important: Those born within a day or two of a sign change will have some characteristics of each sign.

♈

The Aries Man

March 21–April 19

Growing old is inevitable; growing up is optional.

There's something refreshingly honest in the way an Aries man puts his own needs first—at least a woman knows where she stands. And even though he lacks some of the traits we love, like thoughtfulness and unselfishness, he's still mighty hard to resist. The great psychologist, Carl Jung, defined masculinity as "knowing what you want and knowing what you have to do to get it," and that's a perfect description of Aries. If you like a confident, outspoken guy who doesn't pout or get moody, an Aries might be just the one for you.

He can be a hero or a scoundrel, but you have to admire his spirit. He always has something he wants to accomplish and a dream or two percolating away in his brain. It might be to restore a car or build a company, but he has a purpose and he's dedicated to it.

The pioneers who headed west were Aries-types. They wanted to strike it rich in the mines or stake out their own piece of free land, but most of all, they wanted to see what was beyond the horizon and they didn't let even the possibility of death stop them.

An Aries man is a scrapper who fights for what he wants. He can get into a battle of words, a battle against nature, or a battle for the underdog.

He can be an idealist totally dedicated to a dream or an arrogant ass-hole, but he is probably some combination of both.

A quiet or reserved Aries is rare, but if you meet one, don't be fooled. When you get to know him, you'll see his steely determination to do his own thing and the way he brushes off advice like it was a pesky mosquito.

He's a born leader, but he doesn't stop to consider what life is like for the lowly troops. Employees, waitresses, and even his family know this all too well. If an e-mail gets lost, his steak isn't cooked right, or his shirts aren't picked up from the cleaners, he lets his irritation be known.

He's not big on planning ahead. He's so eager to get on with it, he overlooks the details, so he runs out of gas or overdraws his checking account. He likes a challenge and to rely on his own judgment, but he doesn't give enough thought to the consequences of his actions. He goes hiking alone without telling anyone where he's going or when he'll be back. He drives his motorcycle without a helmet or pours gasoline on the campfire to get it going. It's almost as if he wants a crisis so he has something to overcome.

If you're in love with an Aries man, be prepared for conflict because he sometimes creates it just to vent some of his pent-up irritation. But even though he tries to dominate you, he prefers a woman he can't boss around. He wants you to stand up for yourself and give him a challenge.

The unaware Aries man has a scary flaw: it's what he wants but can't have that really lights his fire. In the beginning of a relationship, he's a blast. He pursues you with all his might and knows just how to make you fall in love with him. He's romantic, highly sexed, and pretty much irresistible, but his attention span is short and he doesn't do well with long-term commitments.

Just when you think life has settled into a comfortable routine, his enthusiasm begins to fade and he doesn't spend all his free time with you anymore. You feel rejected and start to pester him about it. Then he *really* feels tied down, a fate worse to him than losing a six-game parlay on the last game. At this point, you have two options: you can lay down strict rules and force him to make promises he can't keep, or you can realize he's just a kid at heart and always will be.

Don't marry an Aries man and expect that your little twosome or family will be enough for him because, like any kid, he wants to play with his friends. Telling him not to is as useless as telling a child not to run by the pool.

All Aries men are sports fanatics who could spend all weekend watching games; that is, if they aren't out participating in them. They love all kinds of competition or speeding around on something with wheels or that goes fast on the water or snow. You may as well accept it at the get-go. Tell yourself when he goes out to play sports or be with the guys, he's not taking something away—you're giving him something he needs. You can try negotiation, but don't count on it to be very satisfying—he'll find a way to win. Every woman married to an Aries needs her own friends to do things with or a hobby she enjoys pursuing alone.

The Aries man with the fragile ego is the one to be careful of. While you're out there being your own woman with your own interests, he might be nursing hurt feelings and start looking around for someone to make him feel big, strong, and smart. Who? Why, someone new and exciting, of course. His impulsiveness doesn't help when temptation comes along—it takes a very committed man to resist.

Some Aries men are chauvinists. In his perfect world, the little woman would wait on him, cook and clean for him, and take care of all his needs . . . and love doing it. These are the ones to avoid or spend years re-training. Every Aries man has dreams and goals that are so important to him he will expect you to help him pursue them while your own needs and goals come in a distant second, so stay strong and never give them up for him.

The Aries male is ordinarily big in everything—his heart, his generosity, and his vision. Yet he can blow up over trivial stuff. His temper is like a match—it flares quickly, then dies down, so he doesn't carry a grudge. Politics can get him fuming because he's infuriated by the stupidity he sees in the world. He's a candidate for road rage because he hates to be challenged. The lower-type Aries takes these traits to the max and is a spoiled brat who throws a temper tantrum when he doesn't get his way—or he's a bully who proves his worth by beating up someone physically or psychologically. Thankfully, most don't go to that extreme.

When he's following his dream, he can accomplish more than anyone. He fights against incredible odds with courage and guts. When he's relaxed and at his playful best, he's a good companion—entertaining, interesting, and fun to talk to. But don't be surprised when he always changes the subject back to himself, because *he's* the most fascinating and interesting person he knows . . . by far!

How to live with an Aries man

Dos:

1. Tell him you love how he stands up for what he believes in.
2. Overlook his occasional unappealing behavior. Keep the big picture in mind.
3. Believe in his dreams, even if it takes longer than you thought.

Don'ts:

1. Don't give commands or ultimatums; it just gets your blood pressure up.
2. Don't expect him to want to spend all his free time with you.
3. Don't expect a calm, peaceful existence. If you can't take a little conflict, leave the Aries guy to someone who can.

♉

The Taurus Man

April 20–May 20

A glass of wine . . . a hot tub . . . and thee.

A Taurus is exactly the kind of man your mom wanted for you—dependable and responsible. You can count on him to keep his word—if he tells you he'll be somewhere, he's there . . . and on time.

He copes with life's inevitable problems better than any sign. When the roof springs a leak the same day he gets laid off, the mail brings a bill from the IRS for $1,500, and the school calls about your son's behavior, a Taurus guy is the one you want to be with. He has a stoic acceptance and, like the Mars Rover, he just keeps on going.

He's like the strong, handsome hero in romantic fiction. He's solid and immovable—like the earth—and there's a certain comfort in that. He also has a sensual quality that's very appealing to women. Plus he's gentle, affectionate, and good with kids.

He can also be a big pain in the ass—but only if he isn't your type.

If you love delightful surprises, attending a fancy event, or spontaneous little trips, better leave the Bull in the pasture smelling the flowers, where he's content. He doesn't like surprises so why would he surprise you? He's uneasy in a room full of strangers, especially if he isn't in comfortable clothes. And spontaneous trips? He won't suggest it; in fact, he hates being asked to go somewhere without ample time to think it over. Even if it's something he enjoys, he needs at least a few hours, if not days, to think about it before *anything* sounds like fun. If you force him to make a quick decision, his answer is no. About trips in general—he'll go, but he doesn't like to live out of a suitcase or sleep in a hotel. At least bring his pillow, if possible.

But . . . if an uncomplicated, steady guy is what you're looking for, Taurus is your man. Interestingly, he often goes for a fiery-type woman who has the spontaneity and imagination he's missing—then he complains when she doesn't want to stay home. It's another of life's little tricks to keep us off-balance with the opposite sex.

He has a lazy streak and he can be a couch potato, especially if he puts on weight from too little exercise. But once he gets started on a project, he doesn't quit until it's done. He'll put in a lawn, paint the house, or tackle the garage. The sense of accomplishment he gets from finishing a job and viewing his handiwork is reward enough for him.

If you love to pick out your man's clothes, remember: he likes to dress for comfort. Buy him loose-cut silk or brushed cotton shirts and soft denim or cotton pants. If you buy him a new robe, thinking he will surely love it, he may prefer his comfortable old one with the hole. If he puts on a suit and tie to take you somewhere, rest assured you mean the world to him.

Noise and discord get to him, so he's irritated when the kids fight. He dislikes a houseful of people buzzing around like flies, so he doesn't particularly enjoy entertaining. In a restaurant, he feels more comfortable with a booth in the back. Don't make him sit at a table in the middle of the room with people breezing by or coming up behind him.

What he does love are long drives in the country or long-distance car trips where he can view the trees, meadows, and cows grazing in the pasture . . . the scenery that heals his soul. He loves to watch golf on TV; its slow pace and acres of green grass and trees are soothing to him.

Yes, dear sisters, if you need variety or even a wee bit of spice in your life, don't settle down with a Taurus man.

One woman told this story about her Taurus boyfriend: EVERY time they finished a meal, he would push back from the table, grin, and say, "Well, that sure ruined my appetite!" She finally ran off with another man and had a mad passionate weekend, breaking up with Mr. Predictable soon after, a rash act to be sure, but it was either that or strangle him the next time he made that comment.

If you like intellectual games and chatter, look elsewhere. He takes what you say literally and speaks quite bluntly himself. You can't discuss psychological or emotional issues with him; he just blocks it out. When you're trying to explain your feelings and he smiles condescendingly and tells you you're being silly, it's not only invalidating, it's infuriating.

As a lover, he's not bad with his slow and steady manner. (When did we ever go for speed in the bedroom?) This is a very physical, earthy sign, and the Taurus man prides himself on his sexual competence. Sex is important to him and not something to be hurried, but he's not the most exciting lover. Once he finds something that works, he sticks with it. The trick is to teach him what you like in the beginning.

Stubborn? Don't ask! This is the man you are *least* likely to change. Nor can you prod him into doing something . . . you may as well push a mule. In the "Be careful what you ask for" category, don't ask for patience or you may just get a Taurus man! He doesn't like change, especially if it involves starting over, as in new job, new relationship, new location. He's not likely to give up on his marriage, even if it's difficult. There's good news and bad news on that front: the good news is he won't throw away his wife and family and home for love. The bad news is, that's no guarantee he won't find sexual satisfaction elsewhere, but at least he's not the type.

He's a meat-and-potatoes guy—how could a Bull be otherwise? If you're a vegetarian, you'll be cooking two meals or adding meat to his portion. If you're a gourmet who likes to experiment with exotic dishes, chances are he'll eat it but he won't rave about it. He prefers simple fare: meat loaf, pot roast, steak.

Pre-nuptial agreements were invented by a Taurus-type mentality; he doesn't want anyone taking his stuff. It's not so much that he's materialistic as attached. If he has to start over, say because of a devastating fire or divorce, he suffers more than any other sign. New things mean nothing; it's the old familiar objects and furniture he wants around him.

Unfortunately, he may think his possessions include you. If anything can goad him into anger, it's a threat to his security, which means his wife and family. If all he lives for is threatened, he loses his whole purpose and, in extreme cases, can turn violent. Then he has no resemblance to the docile creature you thought you knew. Never wave a red flag at a bull unless you're prepared to be gored.

How to live with a Taurus man

Dos:

1. Remember that, to him, a home-cooked meal is an act of love.
2. Appreciate the fact that you have a man with a good chance of remaining faithful.
3. Be aware that he needs some time every week on the couch in front of the TV without having to answer any questions.

Don'ts:

1. Don't expect him to get over it in a minute when he's angry. Give him time.
2. Don't expect him to attend all the social events you want to go to—this is where your friends come in.
3. Don't give your relatives and friends the impression they can drop by any time. He hates people intruding on his space.

♊

The Gemini Man

May 21–June 21

Gemini men are only after one thing—the TV remote.

There isn't a more interesting man in the Zodiac than a Gemini. He was the first one in his group to send photos from his phone, use a TiVo, or attach speakers to his iPod. His nemesis is boredom, so he amuses himself with technology and gadgets. He likes to figure out how things work, and that includes you! He wants you to say something intelligent so he can analyze it and compare it with what *he* thinks or what you said yesterday. He collects useless bits of information so when he remembers the names of your friends, co-workers, and cat, that you hate powdered creamer, and that you read your horoscope every day, he's just adding trivia to his vast collection . . . and you thought he was fascinated with you! When he has something to say on every topic you bring up, it's because he knows so much and likes to hear himself expound on it.

"At last," you think, "a man I can be friends with," and this time, you'd be right. A Gemini man makes a wonderful friend. It's when the delight of friendship turns into the confining embrace of commitment that the going gets, well, iffy. He's not usually the liar and cheat astrology has made him out to be, but he wants to experience everything life has to offer and fears getting tied down in a career or relationship.

Women who have intolerable (to him) emotional demands are his worst nightmare. If you're a homebody whose dream is to settle into a cozy cottage and raise a couple of kids with a guy who brings home a steady paycheck, you'd best keep looking. If you're an independent, busy woman who requires a lot of freedom yourself, a Gemini man is a possibility. If you don't really care about settling down, but do need a lot of your partner's time and attention, you, too, should avoid this sign like the flu.

A Gemini man *may* stick to a job and climb the ladder of success, but he's more likely to duck under the ladder and live by his wits and cleverness. In worst cases, he's a perpetual drifter, forever looking for his true calling. So much is interesting to him and he is good at so many things, how can he decide? Perhaps he could work in his father's business and someday take it over, but if he follows his heart, he'll play in a band on a cruise ship, or stay in a house on Cape Cod while he writes a novel.

If you have a relationship with a Gemini or are considering one, here is something you can expect: you will never have his full attention. Even when he's sitting right there talking to you, he can't help but notice someone who just entered the room. In the time it takes you to utter a sentence, his active mind has touched on a dozen unrelated thoughts. Don't think it means he has lost interest; it's just his natural curiosity. He can actually listen to you *and* a conversation next to him. His mind performs best when it's busy.

True to his twin nature, he often does things in "twos." He has his work and an important hobby, or he has two jobs, or he may work and go to school. He has two cars or two computers, but hopefully not two women, at least not when one of them is you! This "everything in twos" thing is amazing, but you'll see it at work in his life.

Watching TV with him is a trip—good luck prying the remote out of his nimble fingers. All men are compulsive channel-switchers, but a Gemini has to be the worst, because his mind is as quick as his attention span is short. He doesn't want to miss anything and he actually absorbs information best in little bits and pieces, while your own brain circuits are fried.

Life won't be boring if you hook up with a man born under the sign of the Twins because you'll never know what's coming next. You do know that you're dealing with two different personalities? How can you predict what he'll do when you aren't even sure who's in there? He doesn't even like to state his opinions, because he knows they'll change and he instinctively doesn't want to be held to them. Just when you think you know him, he'll adopt a new attitude or get a new plan . . . how confusing is that?

You'd think with all the information he's accumulated, he'd have some knowledge of himself, but he puts so much faith in the intellect, he discounts emotion. He can talk himself into or out of things until he has no feelings left, only arguments—then he comes across as cold or calculating. Even if he knows what his emotional needs are, he won't share with anyone other than his own twin self, his true other half.

Gemini men need to constantly absorb information so they are usually avid readers. Makes one wonder how they survived before the World Wide Web came along and put a whole world of information at their fingertips that they can learn and pass on to the rest of us.

His second necessity is to communicate. He uses his cell phone, e-mail, instant messaging, and live journals to keep in touch. When he's not on the computer or watching TV, he's having a conversation with someone. Don't tell him your darkest secrets, or any piece of news you don't want to get around. He doesn't do it with malicious intent, but he can't help talking about anything interesting . . . unless it's about him! This incurable gossip never tells on himself. If he thinks you're prying into his secrets, he'll be playfully evasive, make a witty comment, and change the subject.

If you are married or considering marriage to a Gemini, you have to be flexible and have faith. Don't try to pin him down to a schedule and tell him he has to mow the lawn every Saturday or have dinner with your folks every Thursday night. Don't get upset if he wants to spend time with his friends playing computer games online. The only way to live with a Gemini man is to trust him. That sounds illogical, but it's true, because you can never catch him in a lie. If you ask too many questions, he'll just lie more. You can't force him to follow your plan and you can't make him want to be with you. You can only accept him as he is. If he isn't faithful, your relationship will deteriorate and you'll know something is wrong.

This man thrives on mental and physical mobility. Tie him down to one place and one job, doing one thing, and eventually he'll leave—or act so outrageously that *you* decide to call it quits. Maybe you'll get an "I'm Sorry" card in the mail. No, too much trouble. He'll send an e-mail.

The worst type of Gemini is a flim-flam man who lies to save himself. He rationalizes his actions so he isn't bothered by guilt or regret. He can cheat or steal, with forgery being one of his specialties. He can talk his way into your bank account, rip through your savings, and trash your credit rating. A Gemini-type is smart enough to juggle two families in different towns and keep everyone fooled, at least for a while. Luckily, these dangerous Geminis are rare.

If you can't trust and respect your lover, then all the great sex and scintillating conversation in the world don't mean a thing, not in the long run, anyway. Go slowly with a Gemini man and let his actions demonstrate his intentions and integrity.

Even the great Gemini men never really grow up because their minds stay young—and curious. They're always changing and they will be different tomorrow than they are today. A woman may not find tranquility with a Twin, but maybe she'll learn something, like how to cherish the moment and let the future take care of itself.

How to live with a Gemini man

Dos:

1. Cultivate a support system so you don't have to depend on him for all your emotional needs.

2. Remember when he argues with you, sometimes it's just because he likes to argue. He can change sides and be just as convincing.

3. Keep up on current events and technology. Improve your computer skills. Be smart!

Don'ts:

1. Don't lecture him about chores and responsibility.

2. Don't get upset when he's always late. He has a lot of fish to fry in any one day.

3. Don't try to keep him off his computer. Get matching computers and join him or find another way to have a pleasurable time.

The Cancer Man

June 22–July 22

Guys have feelings too, but like, who cares?

If you ever dated a Cancer man who didn't call after a pleasant first date, you might have assumed he didn't enjoy it as much as you did. He did, but true to his crab-like tendencies, he's doing his famous "side-step." He hesitates to make the next move until he's sure he won't be rejected, so don't be afraid to call him and suggest another date. He might hesitate again when it comes time to make the final commitment of marriage. A Cancer man has a shell around him for protection—he can be wounded because he feels things so deeply.

In spite of this, most of them do end up married with a family. They want to re-create the supportive home they knew (or longed for) as a child. The Cancer man makes an excellent father, although he can feel threatened if his wife gives most of her attention to the children: he needs reassurance of her love for him. Home, mom, and apple pie—the keys to the Cancer man's heart.

Let's talk about mom. He is always tied, through love or through hate, to his mother. They are either very close, or totally alienated. In either case, she remains an important figure to him. The advice from your mom to "find a man who loves his mother" was never more true than with a Cancer, because the Crab who hates his mother is one crusty crustacean. Better leave him undisturbed in his shell.

You know you've got a good man when he's willing to go shopping or take a yoga class with you. A Cancer man will often make personal sacrifices to please you, like watching the kids while you go for a massage. He's sensitive, sweet, and wants a family as much as you do. When you have to hand him a tissue in a sad movie, you're touched.

Cancer men have a lot of built-in conflict because little boys soon learn that men are supposed to be tough and that showing emotion is weak. Women know this is simplistic, not to mention just plain wrong, but most men feel they must live up to the expectation, so a Cancer man puts on a false front. His most common disguise is the jovial extrovert, but that's not really him—the prickly guy with the soft heart is.

There's a lot of variation in Cancer men, since their ruling planet is the changeable moon. A relatively well-adjusted Cancer from a loving home is far easier to live with than one who has been wounded in childhood. The injured one is always watching and waiting for his greatest fear to come true—that he isn't loved—so he sulks when he feels rejected and gets cranky when he feels unneeded. He can't explain his feelings and doesn't understand them himself, so he withdraws emotionally and sometimes physically to protect himself. When he feels you are no longer totally on his side, he can be cold and even cruel, as if to say, "I've given so much and you don't appreciate me."

Even the well-adjusted Cancer man isn't necessarily sensitive to those outside his circle because it takes time for him to build trust. In the meantime, he might be abrupt and even rude, especially if he feels his family and security are threatened—he protects his own, no matter what. But once someone is inside the gates of his world, he will do anything for them.

All the water signs (Cancer, Scorpio, and Pisces) are complicated because theirs is the realm of feelings, and feelings are partly unconscious. When they are aware of their emotions, they are the most intuitive and psychic of signs. When they are not fully aware of their emotions and motivations, they are overly-sensitive to the slightest threat. A Cancer man needs a woman who understands him, or at least gives him emotional support. Even a woman who isn't especially nurturing will make the effort to give him the love, encouragement, and reassurance he needs, if she's smart. It's a good investment for marriage with a man who will be there for the long haul.

To a Cancer man, just the thought of divorce is horrifying, so even if he's unhappy, he'd rather stay put—he is rarely the one to make the decision to separate. If he does want out, he may goad her into getting fed up so she ends it—then he doesn't have to do the confronting.

Maybe this will help you decide if the Crab is your kind of man: Cancer is one of the signs in the Zodiac most likely to go out there in the world and make something happen! Because he can seem unsure of himself, people often underestimate him, but he has vision and great imagination. He's a good boss because his employees are like family to him and he looks out for their welfare. He is unlikely to change jobs because he likes the security of staying with the same company and people.

He's good with finances. He knows his FICO score and has downloaded his credit report. He watches his money closely, sometimes a little *too* closely. Plan on keeping unnecessary lights turned off and watch your credit card limits. A Cancer man worried about money can be cheaper than the toy in a box of Cracker Jack, but that's why they do well financially—it's a trade-off.

Since he's used to being different in a macho world, he's one man who isn't afraid to pitch in around the house. If he gets home from work first, he might start dinner or unload the dishwasher. He's devoted to his children and listens to his wife. He's understanding and encouraging. He has a crazy, lunar laugh and he isn't afraid to use it. He worries—about money, his health, his parents, his children, his employees. He's the kind of guy we women have been saying we want men to be—nurturing and sensitive.

How to live with a Cancer man

Dos:

1. Love your in-laws and show the proper respect. If you can't love them, fake it, especially with his mom.

2. Encourage him to learn to relax via tapes, yoga, breathing exercises, or meditation. His high-strung nervous system needs it.

3. Tell him how much you admire a man who isn't afraid to show his feelings.

Don'ts:

1. Don't make plans with your friends without talking it over with him first. It's not asking permission, it's just showing him you care about his feelings.

2. Don't tell him to stop dwelling on the past. It's his nature to look back and ponder what could have been or what he might have done differently.

3. Don't force him to give up his old clothes or childhood mementos. If you must clean out, go through your closets together and show him that you're getting rid of your old stuff too.

THE LEO MAN

JULY 23–AUGUST 22

My life is like a jigsaw puzzle
and you're a real important part—
you know, like a corner piece.
—Sam Malone to Rebecca on *Cheers*

The Sun is at its best and strongest in this sign, so there's no man like a Leo man. He's generous, fun, and likely to be a success. All he wants is to be treated like a V.I.P. and loved like a long-awaited only child.

He has style and charisma, not to mention good hair. It's easy to see why he thinks he should be the most important thing in your world and, believe me, he does. He knows how to make you feel feminine and desirable. He will take you to a nice restaurant and give you a lavish gift, but he needs to hear how much you love the gift and adore him—it warms him down to his kingly toes. He gets crotchety if he thinks his grand gestures, and even his small ones, aren't appreciated, so for the love of God, show enthusiasm when he's thoughtful!

He wants to love and be loved. In fact, he doesn't just want it, he needs it! A Leo who doesn't feel loved is a sad and lonely soul and won't stay that way for long, if he can do anything about it—and he usually can because he's so lovable himself. There are few bachelors in this sign.

A Leo will protect his loved ones and do anything for them. He praises his children and encourages them to succeed. He sees only their good qualities and brags about them every chance he gets.

If you're an independent woman with an important career of your own, you have a tightrope to walk with him. The tricky part is being his adoring helpmate and balancing that with your own pursuits. On the one hand, he's proud of you, but on the other hand, he suffers if he thinks he comes in second. A self-confident Leo is okay with an independent and accomplished mate, but a Leo who isn't sure of his own worth is threatened.

As much as he loves to give, he isn't a good receiver of gifts or favors. He has an aura of self-sufficiency and never admits to needing anything or being down. If he's just declared bankruptcy and a friend asks him how things are going, they're always "great." He doesn't allow anyone to feel sorry for him.

A Leo man likes to live large. He has a new home theater delivered when you're wondering how to make the mortgage payment. He's extravagant for two reasons. First, he buys only the best, and second, he resents limitations, so he isn't likely to check the bank balance to see if he can afford it. He doesn't let small details like a budget dictate what he can do. A woman has to have a lot of faith to survive with him.

All Leos aren't extroverts who want to be the center of attention— yours might be the quiet type—but all Leos have a powerful drive to be recognized and to be significant in some way. They want to accomplish something big, and with their vast creativity and willpower, they usually do. Leo often rises to a position higher than what he was born into and is often the recipient of some lucky breaks along the way.

Leo men take responsibility seriously, are good managers, and want to be known for their ability and integrity. They won't ask their employees to do anything they wouldn't do themselves. They complain that they have to carry the whole load, but secretly they love it. They aren't good at delegating responsibility. A Leo boss can tell Jake where to place the chairs, but he can't put him in charge of where to put them.

The Leo man loves gambling and, like everything else, he likes to do it on a large scale. This is especially true if he gambles with friends because his "high roller" image is at stake and it can cloud his usually good judgment. Investing in the stock market is an accepted form of gambling and he will want to have a go at that, as well.

If you have had a failed relationship with a Leo man, you may have tried to change him and discovered you were wasting your time. Or you may have found out that he had you both in hock up to your eyebrows. Or perhaps you realized the only thing you had in common was that you were both in love with him. Actually, his ego is the biggest threat to marriage. If he had a rough start in life and is insecure, a long-lasting relationship is hard to achieve. Once his great love (you) takes on the role of wife, you're the one who sees his faults and that, along with the rough patches all marriages have, is enough to make him look to another woman for the admiration and respect he needs to feel okay about himself. So if you're going for a Leo, find a secure one!

When he gets older and has made his mark on the world, the Leo man still has the best part of his life to look forward to . . . retirement, and becoming a grandfather. A Leo man loves children and has a childlike sense of fun, so his grandchildren naturally adore him. Their unconditional love, plus the excuse to buy toys, makes a decent Leo dad into a phenomenal grandfather.

If your Leo man has faith in himself and can laugh at himself a little, he's one of the good ones.

How to live with a Leo man

Dos:

1. Tell him often how much you love and respect him and how proud you are of him.

2. Go to his office looking fabulous; he needs a mate he is proud of.

3. Fashion your world around him. It's against our code, yes, but there it is.

Don'ts:

1. Don't exchange the gifts he buys you, even if you hate them, unless he says he doesn't mind . . . and even then, don't believe him.

2. Don't correct him in public and, by all means, never belittle him.

3. Don't tell him he's told that story before. Just listen with love and a smile.

THE VIRGO MAN

AUGUST 23–SEPTEMBER 22

Virgo men are like computers. They have a lot of data,
but they're still clueless.

There's a lot to admire in a Virgo man. For one, he can figure out why your computer won't turn on. He can take it apart, diagnose the problem, and put it back together before you can say, "My god, my whole life's on that thing." Just call him the trouble-shooter of the Zodiac. He likes to feel useful so he's happy to help you out, plus it gives him an opportunity to show you how smart he is.

A Virgo man is intelligent and likely to opt for higher education, although he can also be a skilled craftsman. He often has a hobby and he excels at anything that requires logic, manual dexterity, and attention to detail. He likes to feel useful, so he is seldom without a project.

He's good at solving problems, especially yours. Being asked for advice makes his week, because he loves to give his opinion and feel needed. Present him with a dilemma you're having with a co-worker and he'll tell you just what you should do. Although he may not factor in emotions or psychological motivations, he's shrewd and perceptive. Combine his input with your knowledge of people and you can be fairly certain of the best approach to take.

Let's talk about something the sign is famous for—its tendency to criticize. They say a Virgo man notices every little thing that's wrong and (in typical male fashion) takes for granted what's right. If you just washed twenty-seven windows, he notices the one you missed. If you cook a delicious meal, he remarks that the cashew chicken has a tad too much curry. It's the natural result of a mind that can't stop analyzing.

This trait is more pronounced in a Virgo who didn't have the advantage of a loving and supportive home. He always sees the bad, never the good, and always needs to be right. He pushes you to state your opinion just so he can shoot it down with a barrage of facts, and prove you're wrong.

This kind of Virgo asks about the "B" in History when his daughter brings home four "A's." When his fifteen-year-old boy makes the baseball team, he says, "You better start working out, son—you're awfully puny." This is the criticism that crushes the spirit. If you have this kind of Virgo, you have some toughening up to do. Some women have needed therapy to restore their self-worth. Even so, these flaws aren't likely to deliver a fatal blow to a marriage, and if a woman is self-confident, she can live with him, profit from his advice, and ignore the rest.

Virgo is the least flighty and most responsible sign in the Zodiac. He won't spend money foolishly or buy something outrageously expensive—for either of you. Don't expect romance to trump practicality. His gifts to you will be useful—a vacuum cleaner, a set of cookware, maybe a book on low-fat cooking. At least he doesn't make many financial mistakes—he's far too wise to bet the farm and lose it, or make disastrous investments.

Another Virgo trait is the compulsion for cleanliness. He isn't a slob who leaves a trail of popcorn kernels, dirty socks, and old newspapers for you to pick up. If he does, stop doing if for a week and when he sees the mess, he'll quit. And you never have to worry about his personal hygiene—he probably showers *too* often.

You might find a bachelor Virgo who lets dirty dishes pile up in the sink and has to wade through the living room to get to the TV, but deep down, it bothers him.

If a clean house isn't his obsession, something else will be, like keeping his car spotless or hanging each tool in its proper spot. Here is one woman's experience with a Virgo man that illustrates their lack of spontaneity:

One evening they were about to make love. She was in bed, waiting expectantly for him. She watched as he placed his pants on a hanger, *pressed the crease with his fingers,* and then hung them carefully in the closet. Her enthusiasm paled when she realized he wasn't going to be carried away by the throes of passion any time soon.

The term "workaholic" may be overused these days, but it could have been invented for a Virgo. Expect him to spend most of his time at work. A woman who wants him to participate in family life may be disappointed when he doesn't show up for a little league game or a dance recital. He judges himself on how he performs on the job and that's his priority, period. But at least the family won't have to struggle through many lean periods with no paycheck. If a job provides him with security, he won't jump from company to company. If he *is* out of work, he gets depressed and begins to doubt himself. He goes around fixing things that don't need fixing and, in general, giving his wife a glimpse of what to expect when he retires.

Don't be surprised if you give him a chaise lounge for the patio but never see him in it. He has a list of chores for the weekend because there's always something that needs doing. The children of one Virgo man would lock themselves in the bathroom on the weekends just for a few moments of peace.

If you're health-conscious, you will have much in common with him. Give him a fitness club membership you can enjoy together because he really needs to exercise—his nervous system demands it. He's a worrier and if he's not worried about money, he worries about his health. He probably takes vitamins, watches his diet, and flosses his teeth.

The typical Virgo is finicky about what he wears. This becomes apparent as early as the toddler stage. Tim, a two-year-old Virgo, called the clothes he didn't like "grumpy," and flat-out refused to wear them. According to little Tim, most of his wardrobe was "grumpy," especially the clothes bought at the discount store. Even at that age he wouldn't settle for less than comfort and quality, at least not without a fight.

To his credit, a Virgo man will take care of you when you're sick (if he's not at work, that is). He understands being of service and will do it stoically and efficiently.

Never say anything bad about him or anything good, for that matter—just leave him out of it. He's a private person who doesn't like attention; sometimes even a compliment makes him uncomfortable.

He doesn't want to be embarrassed in public so don't hang on him, pat his butt, or even sit too close. He prefers to keep all expressions of love private. In bed, he may not be the most creative, but he is a good technician and prides himself on being efficient. You could do worse.

How to live with a Virgo man

Dos:

1. Let him do all the repairs and remodeling he wants and pretend not to notice if it's not perfect. He knows.

2. Smell delicious at all times.

3. Remember he will mellow after his 30s or 40s and become more attuned to family.

Don'ts:

1. Don't underestimate the importance of his job. He can be thrown for a loop if there are any unforeseen changes at work.

2. Don't get angry when he says, "I told you so." No doubt he did.

3. Don't pick out clothes for him unless you're sure of his likes and dislikes—he's very particular, in case you haven't noticed.

♏

The Scorpio Man
October 23–November 21

Women are looking for a mate.
A Scorpio man is looking to mate.

So you're attracted to a Scorpio man and you want to get to know the real him so you two lovebirds can share. Gee, that's sweet—but give up the dream—he's harder to read than a Chinese newspaper and he never shares his inner self.

It's not just that he keeps secrets, he thrives on them! He likes to know something you don't. Some of them have separate friends who don't know the others exist. Some have a mysterious past no one knows about.

He maintains control by keeping a lid on his emotions, so he carries a lot of emotional baggage. You might hear him casually mention something that happened in his childhood and you realize the pain is as raw as when it happened.

One Scorpio boy was repeatedly hurt and angry when his father promised every summer to build him a tree house, but never did. It wasn't just the tree house, it was losing trust in his dad. He carried that pain into adulthood and held it against his father. He finally admitted it to him thirty years later!

The Scorpio man's strong opinions and passionate likes and dislikes, combined with the male ego, can be a fearsome combination. If you're a peace-loving woman, it's going to be tough because blow-ups are fairly common with him. You'll wonder why he gets himself so worked up over trifles. He tries to be the policeman of the world and wants everyone to see the error of their ways and, hopefully, pay for them. He can't just let things go, especially if it concerns his self-respect, so is it any wonder he loves and hates with such passion? A Scorpio man loves very few, perhaps only one true love in a lifetime.

This sign has the worst reputation and is the most misunderstood of any in the Zodiac. One reason is they refuse to play society's games. A Scorpio man doesn't care if people like him so he doesn't schmooze and make nice just to get along. If someone tells a joke and he doesn't think it's funny, he just stands there with a stone face and a gaze that says, "You poor fool."

If he's injured by an innocent remark, he can wait for years to get even. Case in point: Marisa got after Scott, her Scorpio cousin, for calling too late one night and told him, "Don't call me after ten." One night, four years later, Scott's mother, Marisa's aunt, died. Marisa didn't find out about her aunt until the next day.

"Why didn't you call me?" she asked him.

"You told me not to call you after ten."

That's the sting of the Scorpion.

A Scorpio man is impossible to overlook. His sheer animal magnetism attracts many an unwary female, but even though he's complicated, he can be well worth the trouble, as long as you know a few things in advance.

For starters, he's intensely loyal. Once he's your friend, you have a friend for life. That isn't to say he won't ever screw around on you, but real loyalty, to him, is far more important than mere physical faithfulness. See? He's complicated. And yes, he loves sex, but that's because he's a man, not a Scorpio. If sex means more to him, it's because he takes it so seriously. It means being vulnerable and letting someone know something about him they can use against him someday. Scorpio men can do without sex, but they can never do without feeling vitally connected to someone or some thing.

He has a code of honor he lives by—if it kills him—and his code includes not letting anyone get the best of him. If it means hurting himself to stand up for a principle or to get even, he will pay the price. You may as well save your breath than try to talk sense into him. Those fanatics who go to jail rather than pay income tax? Scorpio planets, you can bet on it.

One Scorpio man couldn't get satisfaction from a mechanic who overcharged for inferior work, so he stood out in front of the business for three days holding a sign and handing out flyers announcing their shoddy practices.

Another Scorpio, employed in the office of a lawn care company, got fed up with an irate customer who accused him personally for inadequate service. One night he paid a visit to the customer's yard and left a present—seed from a noxious weed that spreads and cannot be eradicated without digging up all the grass.

One Scorpio guy has a grudge against the English language! When he discovered all the exceptions to the rules and that there are words like fare and fair that sound alike but have different meanings, he declared, "Well that's just stupid!" and thereafter refused to learn it.

No matter to what depths he sinks, you can never count him out. Like Rocky or Clinton, he can always make a comeback and reinvent himself. He can create a new life, adopt totally different values and goals or recover from a life-threatening illness like Lance Armstrong, who has a Scorpio Ascendant. That's the real power of Scorpio.

What about the famous Scorpio jealousy? Someone once said having a Scorpio lover makes you feel like a bowling ball. A Scorpio man *can* learn to trust you, but it takes oh, five or ten years. Don't be surprised to find out he's been following you to check that you were where you said you'd be. Scorpio men are all private investigators at heart and spying is one of their favorite games.

Never use jealousy to spark his interest, and don't talk about your ex-lovers—it will backfire. Even if he says he's okay with it, don't believe him! Play it straight with this guy. If he is crossed, he will get even, however long it takes, so you are wise to proceed with caution.

Noble or higher-type Scorpios are called Eagles and they can make a real contribution to society. The scary ones are the Snakes and you don't want to mess with one of those. They have been badly injured in childhood and have never healed. If they are betrayed or their mate wants to leave, they can hate just as passionately as they once loved. A Snake will find a way to get even like vandalizing your car, running up credit cards in your name, or putting your private photos on the Internet. At his worst, he can even be violent. Sometimes the only satisfaction is in knowing his deeds will come back to bite him in the butt eventually.

His willpower is immense. He brings a passion to everything in his life and he can drive himself to work to the point of exhaustion. One thing is for sure if you dance with a Scorpio man: you will never forget him.

How to live with a Scorpio man

Dos:

1. Realize he is what he is and he won't change to suit you.

2. Vow to yourself that you will never be unfaithful or even tell him an untruth.

3. Remember that a Snake can become an Eagle, but only because he has decided within himself to do so.

Don'ts:

1. Don't tell your friends one iota of his personal business. If he finds out you violated his privacy, he'll never forgive you or trust you.

2. Don't pry into his feelings, his past, his life. You won't learn anything and he will only become more secretive.

3. Don't expect to hear "I'm sorry" very darn often. Humility isn't in his repertoire.

The Sagittarius Man

November 22–December 21

If at first you don't succeed,
skydiving isn't for you.

Why does a Sagittarian man stray? Because he can. Women are naturally attracted to his fun-loving, outgoing personality, so he often finds himself facing temptation. It's no comfort to know that Donald Trump has a Sagittarian Moon. Real self-centered Sagittarians cannot commit to just one woman. They need a crowd to play to and love to be the center of attention.

But don't think every Sagittarius man will be unfaithful—sweeping statements like that are just silly. Did you read the Prologue at the beginning of Part One? If not, here's the gist of it. Most people are a combination of five to eight signs so there's no such thing as a 100 percent *anything*. A Saj with a Cancer Moon is a much different animal that a Saj with an Aries Moon, so take this as a guide but don't get paranoid. Now on to what a 100 percent Sagittarius man is all about.

He's famous for being easily bored—and he wants to be constantly learning. He likes to meet people because they're interesting and they teach him stuff. He can be a social climber and likes to have important and prestigious friends. He actually has a big turnover in the friend department because he drops names off his list as quickly as he adds new ones.

Sports and freedom are his hot buttons. Many of them would rather be participating in or watching sports with their friends than have a close relationship with a woman. It's easy to see why the Sagittarius man has a hard time settling down in one place and becoming the responsible, dependable guy most women are looking for.

He has one trait that makes it less likely that he will wander and that's the way he won't fall for another woman so hard that he is willing to mess up his life just to have her. Aries and Leo can do that, but Sagittarius isn't burdened with the emotions or impulsiveness that would cause him to fall in love, deeply and forever. This can be good news or bad news, depending on if the woman is you!

Anyway, Sagittarius is called the Bachelor of the Zodiac for all of the above reasons. Some women are convinced that the only true love a Saj man ever really has is his dog! If you're involved with an Archer, it does absolutely no good to become the jealous, suspicious lover. Crying and complaining are counter-productive, so try changing your response: Make plans with your friends, follow your own dreams, and enjoy life the way he does. If you're lucky enough to get a Sagittarian willing to make a commitment, don't think for a minute that you've tamed him: he'll never adjust to being tied to your agenda.

There are many reasons why a Saj man is irresistible, especially if you long for excitement and adventure. He loves to travel and see new places—it's one way he gains knowledge, so keep your overnight bag handy and try to love whatever new interest he conjures up. He's quick with a laugh, generous to a fault, and almost always in a good mood—the party really doesn't start until he arrives.

Ever the optimist, he has five reasons why his team is going to win or why his new job is going to be the best one yet. His enthusiasm is catching and sure makes it hard for a girl to keep a clear head. You won't have to cheer him up because he's seldom down. He has a child-like belief that everything will turn out okay. Walt Disney was a perfect example of a Sagittarius. He combined animals and comedy—two things Sagittarians love—and there was always a happy ending.

Don't expect him to be sympathetic when you have troubles be-cause he doesn't like to be brought down. A chirpy "Cheer up" may be the closest thing you get to compassion, as the following true story illustrates:

It happened in 2003 in a northern state, during one of the worst blizzards in years. The Nelsons (not their real name) were expecting. In fact, Mrs. Nelson was in labor, and as the storm increased in intensity, so did her labor pains. They called 911, but by then their street was snowbound and closed to traffic. The rescuers decided the only way to get her to a hospital was on a snowmobile. Just imagine, dear sisters, what that would be like. It's hard enough to lie on a *bed* during labor, much less bounce on the back of a snowmobile! But *Mr.* Nelson was fearless. Here's what he said on national TV:

"I wasn't worried. When I heard they were bringing in the snow-mobiles, it really excited me. I love the snow!" Looking for sensitivity in a Saj man? You may as well look for maturity in a three-year-old.

To give Mr. Nelson the benefit of the doubt, he may have been truly concerned that his wife was going to the hospital on a snowmo-bile, but it just goes to show how they always see the bright side.

A Sagittarian does everything in a big way. Moderation? What's that? When he's buying you a diamond, well okay, but when he invests all his money on a sure-thing stock and it tanks, it's a disaster. If he goes to the store, better clean out the cupboards, cuz he'll bring home the giant size of everything. At least he doesn't haggle over trifles and he doesn't fumble around when the check arrives at a restaurant; he often picks it up for everyone whether or not he can afford it.

Sagittarius is the sports nut of the Zodiac. With him, it's not a choice; he absolutely *needs* sports in his life, either active or spectator, usually both. Most Saj men love outdoor life; skiing, hiking, rock climbing, whitewater rafting, etc. If you share his interests and can par-ticipate, it's a beautiful thing, because he sure won't give them up for you.

Even if he's not that physically active, he reads about sports or watches them on TV. When he says, "Honey, you're working too hard," he really means, "I can't hear the game over the vacuum cleaner!" If you complain or nag him about it, he'll just go somewhere else. However, a Sagittarius man isn't just a big hunk of happy humanity watching sports. At his best, he's an idealist who believes in the laws of the land and wants to do the right thing. He has high morals and loves education, either formal or that which he pursues on his own. At his worst, he's an irresponsible bum who wants everything and wants it now.

If you're looking for a reliable guy who makes a disciplined effort and is always there for you, look elsewhere, but don't expect the magic you'll experience with a Saj. He may take you on a wild ride, but, hey, life is short, you know?

How to live with a Sagittarius man

Dos:

1. Let him run the errands while you pay the bills—he's much happier being on the go.

2. Encourage him to take the job that allows him a flexible schedule.

3. Respect his right to sit back with a beer and enjoy the game in peace.

Don'ts:

1. Don't expect him to keep all his grandiose promises.

2. Don't try to make him adhere to a rigid schedule.

3. Don't ever ask him, "Honey, do these pants make me look fat?"

The Capricorn Man

December 22–January 19

Coffee, chocolate, Capricorn men . . . some things are just better rich.

If a responsible, hard-working guy is your ideal, you need look no further than a Capricorn man. If he doesn't have money now, there's a good chance he will in the future. It takes time for this sign to come into its own, so when he's young, he might not be as stable and hard-working as he will be later on. He may well have had responsibilities at a young age, so during his early adult years, he might try out different lifestyles. But, eventually, he'll settle down and be known as hard-working, even ambitious, and he won't have much respect for people who aren't.

Since he's into security and getting ahead, how can he be anything but careful with money? He's responsible to his creditors and doesn't spend more than he should—and the older he gets, the more interested he becomes in saving and investing for the future. He's not cheap in the usual sense because he values quality. He wants to see you in classy, expensive clothes, but he's uncomfortable when you spend money acquiring them. It's a sticky wicket. The worst types are downright stingy.

He can discipline himself to reach his goal and, as his partner, he will expect you to do everything in your power to help. It may be as a working woman in your own right or helping him in the family business, but a homemaker-wife is equally valuable. He thinks of parties as opportunities to network and promote himself, so a good hostess is an asset.

They say the more a man is involved with his career and the more responsibility he has, the harder he is to live with, so naturally he isn't going to be all fun and games. Some Capricorn men don't have time for things like having fun or taking a vacation. If your guy is like that, don't depend on him alone for companionship.

Capricorn men often prefer older women who are more serious. Even in their youth, they appreciate age, look up to authority figures, and enjoy older friends. When they become part of the older generation, they say things like, "What are kids coming to these days?" or "As you sow, so shall you reap," or "Use it up, wear it out, make it do," and cute stuff like that. Life is serious business for a Capricorn.

He values family life and loves his children, but he knows how to set firm limits. He likes the idea of a chart so their mother can check off each chore when it's completed. The kids will grow up to either respect authority or rebel against it, depending on their personalities and how inflexible he has been. He also expects his wife to adhere to all his "shoulds" and "should nots." He would like to have a chart of chores for her, too, but even he knows that would be carrying it too far.

The more rigid Capricorn men are impossible to negotiate with. They're the ones who say, "This is what I want you to do," or "This is how it has to be." Some women like to be told, "Don't worry, I'll take care of it." But if they don't understand their finances, investments, and retirement plans, they will have a difficult time if they ever have to handle everything themselves.

A Capricorn man is so sure that his way is the only way he doesn't realize that people can have different opinions and still be right. He has definite ideas and when other people's desires or lifestyles differ from the "right" ones, he has a hard time accepting it. Some Capricorn men have even disowned a grown son or daughter who refused to follow his rules and stepped on his principles or morals.

Somewhere in middle age, a Capricorn man notices that he's missed out on a lot of joy in life. Even though he longs for security, he also longs for emotional fulfillment. Maybe he's made his mark in the world or maybe he's given up some of his loftier goals, but he realizes his wife and children are as important as work and he chooses to spend more time with them. Either that, or he goes through the "middle-age crazies," and acts totally out of character for a monogamous-minded guy like him. He might make new friends, buy a perkier wardrobe, and find a younger woman. The more daring Goat might even have liposuction on his love handles or have the bags under his eyes removed.

But even when he's doing the crazy thing, he keeps an eye on the bottom line. He's capable of passion and he likes the idea of romance, but he won't sacrifice everything he has worked so hard for just for love. Even if his wife divorces him, he's too shrewd to lose financially. Whichever path he takes, devoted family man or trophy-wife seeker, he seems to get younger as he ages: Cary Grant and George Burns were both Capricorns.

A Capricorn man is usually healthy. He has a lot of strength and stamina because he's built to last, although arthritis may get him at some point. His symbolic lesson is to learn to bend—hence, the stiff joints. Unlike many signs, he will go to the doctor when he's concerned about his health because he's courageous in facing up to problems, but he doesn't want anyone fussing over him.

If you're the type who wants and needs support, a Capricorn man will be protective and a great source of wisdom. But if you want to be your own woman and make decisions for yourself, you may lock horns with him because he doesn't give in and he isn't easily dominated.

How to live with a Capricorn man
Dos:

1. Take his advice in most things. Frustrating as it is, he's usually right.

2. If you want him around a lot, encourage him to have a home office.

3. Appreciate his devotion to family, even if your in-laws get to you at times.

Don'ts:

1. Don't run up the credit cards; he hates being in debt. Be thankful you'll probably never have to declare bankruptcy.

2. Don't lose his respect by making foolish choices that screw things up.

3. Don't undermine his discipline of the children; they will profit from it.

The Aquarius Man

Wanted: meaningful overnight relationship.

If you like someone who marches to the beat of a different drummer, an Aquarius man is for you; in fact, his whole band is weird! You'll find him wherever his friends are, because they come as part of the package. Don't underestimate their importance to him; they may be your greatest competition. If you're the type who values privacy, having his friends around so much could become tiresome, if not downright irritating. Plus, if you don't hit it off with them, the party's over before it's begun.

He values friendship more than love, because it's less complicated. He doesn't understand why women need to hear "I love you" so often—he's too impersonal for that. He's attracted to intellectually stimulating women, not those who need emotional support and reassurance. He values his freedom and if you do too, you won't expect him to be there every minute. To the independent woman who already has a busy life, he's a breath of fresh air.

He's intensely curious, especially about anything strange or unusual. If you want someone who will listen to your theories about crop circles, UFOs, or astrology, chances are he will.

He beats out even a Gemini man the way he keeps up with the latest electronic gadgets and fancy technology. He knows how to download music from iTunes or stream a performance from NBC. The Internet is his lifeline to keep in touch with the whole world of ideas and people.

Some Aquarians are fairly conservative and some are way out there, but there is always something different about them. You can spot the Aquarius man at a party; he's the one in a suit and cowboy boots. He's an independent thinker who doesn't go along just to get along—in fact, he prefers to stand out from the crowd. Here's a little test to determine if you have a true Aquarian on your hands. Just tell him he's a little weird. If he smiles in a self-satisfied sort of way, he's an Aquarian and you just paid him a compliment!

If he has a mundane job, he has an unusual way of doing it or he brings something new to the workplace. Or, he has a unique hobby. He's a joiner who gets involved in a cause because he wants his life to make a difference in the world somehow—or maybe he's just looking for kindred spirits—but his schedule is always packed.

You may as well accept the fact that Aquarian men don't domesticate well; in fact, many of them aren't interested in marriage. If he does decide to marry, he's the type who proposes on a billboard or on the Jumbotron at a baseball game. He wants to get married on top of a mountain or on a boat. A woman who hooks up with him will have to deal with the unexpected. He might want to build a log cabin in Montana and, when he gets tired of that, he wants to move to Las Vegas. Then he imagines what it would be like to be the keeper of a lighthouse so he goes to Maine to find out. He likes to visit new places so he can learn about them. His preferred occupation involves travel. If he's confined to a boring routine in one place, he eventually rebels and has to get out.

He may love you to pieces, but he won't show it very often—he sees no reason for flattery and compliments. He usually tells the truth because he doesn't know how to pretty it up. Some Aquarian men can be cold and quite insensitive, but most are sincere and loyal, so if he promises fidelity, he likely will be faithful—not always, but often. If romance is *your* big ticket item, skip Aquarius and try Leo, Pisces, or

Libra. Nevertheless, an Aquarian guy is a friend to cherish. He will give you good advice and listen to your problems. You can discuss things with him and enjoy his companionship.

The old joke about Aquarius is that he loves humanity but doesn't like people. He stands up for an ideal or a principle, but he doesn't have much of a clue when it comes to people's feelings. He's the expert writing a book about relationships who goes to Barnes & Noble to pick up a book he ordered. When it hasn't come in yet, he stomps out in a huff, not caring that he just insulted the woman behind the counter.

He can expound on the issue of equality, but expect his wife to do all the housework—or he makes a case for family values and togetherness, but fails to show up at his daughter's soccer game.

He's funny and is the life of the party, but his humor can have a sarcastic edge. You might wince at some of the things he says, like the guy who referred to a couple's large family as a litter. He likes to meet people, but enjoys making fun of them later—he just likes to talk and laugh and express his opinions, which, by the way, he won't change to please anyone. He *will* change his mind, but then he holds his new opinion just as adamantly . . . until he changes it once more. But don't confuse his actual opinion with the way he switches sides just for the sake of argument. Got that? Well, neither did anyone else. People can't figure him out, and he likes it that way!

Aquarius is the sign of genius. Astrology lore says there are more Aquarians with Nobel Prizes *and* in mental institutions than any other sign. He has been called "half Albert Schweitzer and half Mickey Mouse." He may be a crazy, wacky guy, but he's an original!

How to live with an Aquarius man
Dos:

1. Realize when he says he wants a change, it's not going to be the living room drapes.

2. Know that he needs a safe haven to return to.

3. Understand it's easier for him to state his opinions to many than to say "I love you" to one.

Don'ts:

1. Don't expect him to sugar-coat the truth to spare your feelings.

2. Don't try to win a debate with him.

3. Don't expect him to be the same tomorrow as he is today, or to want the same thing.

THE PISCES MAN

FEBRUARY 19–MARCH 20

How can I miss you . . . if you don't go away?

It's not easy to figure a Pisces man. Like the ocean, he has mysterious depths where strange things live. Pisces is the twelfth and last sign of the Zodiac, and his personality contains part of each of the eleven signs that came before—no wonder he's as complicated as the IRS code.

He's a romantic like Leo, but without the ego. He's a clown like Sagittarius, but his makeup includes a sad tear on his cheek.

He wants to save the world like Aquarius, but on a more personal level. He's sensitive like Cancer, but more open, and he holds onto pain like Scorpio, but doesn't try to get even.

Like Capricorn, he can bide his time and wait for a more hopeful future, but he lacks the Goat's ambition. He's a chameleon like Gemini and adapts like a Virgo, but he's much more complicated than either of them.

He's gentle like Taurus, but not as practical, and he's lovable like Libra, but not as social. Who *is* this guy? The fact is, there is no *real* him. He's all these people and then some; a virtual cast of thousands. You can swim with a Fish but never get hold of him, much less understand him. If you're a down-to-earth sign like Taurus, Virgo, or Capricorn, his ambivalence will drive you crazy. If you're a logical thinker like Gemini or Libra, you'll be stymied by his mysterious thought processes. He can dampen the enthusiasm of Leo and Aries like a barrel of cold water dumped on a winning coach.

A Pisces man seems to be the one you've been waiting for, no matter what kind of man that is. He's a natural actor and he knows how to win your heart. He buys you a rose and takes you to a romantic little place where he looks into your eyes and listens to what's in your heart. He has great insight, not to mention beautiful eyes. He's funny and keeps you laughing, and when he's playing the clown, you mistake him for a lighthearted, carefree type. Wrong. Nothing is that simple with a Pisces man. He has so much going on beneath the surface you will never understand him . . . and neither will he.

He's a deep thinker, a sensitive lover and, at his best, a spiritual soul. But he looks for a strong woman who can help him decide what to do next in life. He needs a lot of emotional and even financial support while he gets his act together. He has gobs of talent, but he lacks confidence and staying power. It's hard for him to set a course because, like a fish, he can't see what's straight ahead so he gets confused—he also gets bored more easily than any other sign.

He doesn't seek the limelight and is often found working behind the scenes in some context. He's also good in the helping professions: he understands people's pain because he carries so much of his own.

There is something about Pisces that seems to draw misfortune. There is often some adversity he has had to overcome and, by doing so, he has developed inner resources.

The injured ones who are bitter or have been betrayed can be treacherous game players. Many a woman has been badly hurt by a Pisces man because she didn't realize she was participating in the self-created drama of his life. You might meet him in a bar looking for pity and sympathy, the victim of a wife who "doesn't understand me."

An illicit affair is appealing to him because of the secrecy and romance and because he needs an escape from day-to-day life. If you find out, he'll say it meant nothing, and that's probably true—but it doesn't hurt any less.

If a sensitive Pisces is brutalized, he may turn to cruelty. These are the most dangerous kind of Fish. Hopefully, you never run into one.

Even normal Pisceans can use drugs and alcohol as escape mechanisms. Some ultimately turn to spirituality, but all are longing to find a better place when life becomes too harsh. The thing that works against Pisces when it comes to addictions is that they tend to do everything to excess. Like tropical fish with food, they just don't know how to set limits.

If you need someone to bail you out, call a Pisces—he feels for anyone down on her luck. That's one thing about him: He gives his money and time and goes out of his way to do favors for anyone, without a second thought. All too often, the very person who has enjoyed his help (not you, of course) turns against him or insults him. Then, when he's given his last dollar to one more ungrateful loser, he says "Oh well. He probably needed it more than I do." If his boss criticizes or demotes him, or his best friend dumps him, he takes it philosophically, almost as if he expects to be taken advantage of or cheated. There's a touch of the martyr in this man, but you have to admire his generosity.

Just because he won't stand and fight, don't think for a moment he can be dominated, because he has his own way of getting what he wants. If you try to pin him down you may find he has simply drifted away —no note, no phone call, just gone, like a fish swimming silently into the depths.

How to live with a Pisces man
Dos:

1. Be alert to signs of alcoholism or drug dependence—his favorite escapes.

2. Accept the many faces of Pisces and remember . . . he won't be the same tomorrow.

3. Try to catch a glimpse of his vision and believe in his dreams.

Don'ts:

1. Don't pressure him for a logical explanation; he knows what he knows.

2. Don't try to fix everything for him; let him work out his own problems.

3. Don't expect him to necessarily take the best-paying job—he has other considerations that are just as important to him.

☆ ☆ ☆ ☆ ☆ ☆ ☆ ☆ ☆ ☆ ☆ ☆ ☆ ☆ ☆ ☆

PART TWO: ALL ABOUT YOU

Your basic nature, what you need
in a relationship, and how your sign
goes with all twelve signs

☆ ☆ ☆ ☆ ☆ ☆ ☆ ☆ ☆ ☆ ☆ ☆ ☆ ☆ ☆ ☆

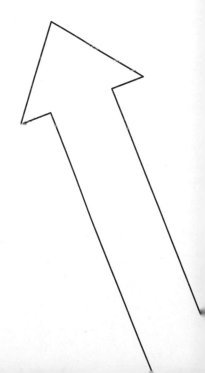

PROLOGUE

WHAT DO *you* NEED IN A RELATIONSHIP?

You can learn a lot about yourself by understanding your basic nature as shown by your Sun sign—it helps you zero in on what you need in a relationship, what makes you happy, and what you just can't stand. We're all different—you might not even notice something that would drive *me* crazy and vice versa.

Read the following paragraphs for your Sun sign. If you know the sign of your Moon or Ascendant, read those as well, for more information.

What if you find out your relationship is hopeless? Not to worry. Even unlikely combinations can work when each person overlooks the differences and quirky traits of the other and is motivated to keep going in spite of them.

Every couple is unique, and no matter how well they get along, their relationship will encounter some thorny patches. Interestingly, the majority of relationships are between signs with the least in common. Why? Perhaps because people are drawn to one another for a purpose. In astrology, relationships have more to do with Saturn, the Teacher, than with Venus, the planet of Love. If we expect the biggest value we get from a relationship is self-knowledge, we won't be disappointed to find it isn't all fun and romance.

The ultimate fate of any relationship is up to the parties involved, and with luck, self awareness, love, and commitment, all combinations are possible.

The Aries Woman
March 21–April 19

An Aries baby had a mind of her own from the first time she peeked out from her pink blanket. She knew what she wanted and she let her parents know—loudly and frequently.

As a toddler, she was as determined as ever. Even after the terrible twos, she continued to insist on her own way, although her cheerful nature returned as soon as she got it.

As a young girl, she expected to be first and best at every game. She made up the rules and told the other kids what to do. She was a tomboy who rode her bike, climbed trees, and, instead of the girls, she played with the boys. If they didn't like it, she told them to shut up.

In high school, she bragged that she could get any boy she wanted, and sometimes she went after a boy just to prove it. She was phoning boys before society decided it was okay.

She got her first job as a teenager and left home at a young age to start her new life. She was happy to finally make her own decisions and no one has told her what to do since.

An Aries woman is outgoing and friendly to everyone, but she doesn't hesitate to tell a co-worker, a rude clerk, or a pushy salesman to shove it. If she had a title, it would be, "Least Likely to Take Shit."

She's independent, frank, and funny—she doesn't make everybody happy and she doesn't care.

Most girls are raised to be nice, so when she voices her opinion, people are taken aback. Her confidence either empowers other women or offends them, usually the latter, so she isn't close to many women. In fact, she still likes to hang with the boys.

She believes people can pull themselves up by their bootstraps, and has little sympathy for weak souls who can't or won't. When she loses her inhibitions, her repressed anger and bitchiness come out and everyone runs for cover.

She fought to get established in her career, she fought to maintain her identity after marriage, and she fought to get back her confidence after a divorce. She used her career as an outlet when she had problems with men, so she was a tireless worker.

She's had lots of relationships—some short-lived, and at least one marriage. She began every one with stars in her eyes, believing she had finally found "the one." She gave it her best, but when it didn't work out and fights over money, in-laws, etc. were never-ending, she cut her losses and moved on. "Life is too short to be unhappy," she says.

It wasn't until her thirties that she figured out what she really wanted in life—and in a husband. If she was married, they had a partnership: they both had careers and shared the work at home.

As a mature woman, she knows she's made mistakes, especially with men. She's aware of how she uses her anger to control or punish. She still thinks she knows best, but now that she realizes she can be brusque and impatient, she's learning to listen and be more thoughtful of people's feelings.

If she's single, she's okay with it. She's won some battles and lost some, but she knows she can take care of herself. She's still as gutsy as ever, she still needs a challenge, and, in spite of everything that's happened to her, she's still optimistic. She fully expects to find the right man, that special guy who lets her be herself.

The Aries woman in love . . .

with another Aries:

When two Rams get together, stand back, something may explode at any moment! They both like to express their opinions and love a fast-paced conversation, each interrupting the other to bring the subject back to themselves.

When the passion has calmed down, they each make the unsettling discovery that the other one thinks they are the boss. But remember, the picture of two Rams with their horns locked in mortal combat are two males. It's a different story when one of them is female.

She isn't above acting helpless to get him to gas up her car, wash the dog, or settle a dispute with the landlord. She's fully capable of doing these things herself, but she likes a man to do her bidding; it's her way of testing to see if he loves her.

Neither wants to give in, so it's surprising how happy these two can be in spite of their power struggles. An Aries man appreciates her independence—he doesn't need her at his side every minute. She's pleased to find a man who is confident and not intimidated by her strength, although she still tries to control him.

They will encounter situations where their goals conflict. If the competition between them gets fierce, the only hope is that one of them is wise enough to compromise. That would be her, usually. But that doesn't mean she gives in, she'll just use a different tactic, leaving him to exult in his imaginary victory.

If they are committed to each other, they can find a way to make it work, but it will require sincere effort and a lot of negotiation. But who else is as bold and daring and interesting as another Aries?

with a Taurus:

The strong, silent type intrigues an Aries woman. A Taurus man is reserved, almost shy, with an easy confidence that's very masculine. The magnetic attraction is so powerful neither will realize, for the longest time, that their relationship is based largely on sex.

His easy-going nature is tested if she flirts with other men—he's very possessive about what he considers his. It's terribly old-fashioned of him, but he guards and protects everything that belongs to him, even people. She's the original feminist and is appalled at being thought of as someone's property. She doesn't have a lot of patience with silly stunts like that; they annoy her.

The way they live is different. He likes to be comfortable and have his favorite things around him—he's kind of a fuddy-duddy that way. She's the opposite. She always has something going on—a meeting, a group, an appointment, a class. She's bored out of her skull if he runs true-to-type and is a homebody.

She exudes charm and femininity, but underneath is a strong will. She enjoys the occasional little argument or back-and-forth bickering episode to clear the air; it vents some of her pent-up anger. A Taurus man isn't comfortable with quarrels; he needs peace and harmony. Living with a dynamo like her is hard on his nervous system.

She takes the lead in this relationship, and it's up to him if he wants to follow.

with a Gemini:

She may not be the easiest to get along with—but she just might be the most exciting woman a Gemini has ever been with. They're both busy, busy, busy all day long. They like to be around people and can be found where the action is. He enjoys the intellectual stimulation and she enjoys the attention. A fun date for them is going to a party, then stopping for a cappuccino, heading home, and talking into the wee hours.

If they take on a joint project, they complement each other's talents and work together well, as long as he doesn't mind doing things her way, which he usually doesn't. His ideas spark her creativity and together they come up with something better than either would alone. Both are natural salespersons and, between them, they can corner the market in their little niche.

An Aries woman feels passionate about what she believes in and wants to get out there and make things happen. She can't understand why he doesn't get as involved or feel as strongly as she does, but his interest usually goes no further than thinking and talking about an injustice. He seldom wants to dig in and do the hard work, so he sometimes comes across as uncaring or insincere.

They make great friends, even if they don't have the intensity for a more serious relationship. If they break up, neither is particularly hampered by guilt or regrets; they both take life as it comes and figure tomorrow is another day. She's too busy deciding where she goes from here, and he's never been the type to worry about mistakes.

with a Cancer:

If these two signs ever managed a long-term relationship, they stayed together in *spite* of their personalities, not *because* of them. Or maybe it was for the kids. Anyway, a Cancer man is too thin-skinned for an Aries woman. She doesn't shade the truth to spare his feelings and if she *does* offend him, she isn't the most sympathetic woman in the Zodiac. She doesn't have the time nor the inclination to indulge a too-sensitive man who doesn't know, or won't say, what's wrong. Eventually, his moods and sulks become one big pain in the ass to her.

One couple with these signs was struggling to make their marriage work because they didn't understand each other's needs. Once, when he was sick, he expected her to take care of him like mom used to do. Instead, she treated him the way *she* wants to be treated when she's sick . . . she left him alone. Of course, he was utterly crushed.

When she's on a whirlwind campaign to get rid of junk, she donates his old clothes and other various items he has squirreled away to the thrift shop without his permission. Even though this is the only way she'll ever get rid of them, she does it at the peril of the relationship.

If she's in a phase where she's in touch with her femininity, she cooks gourmet dinners, scrubs the house from top to bottom, and plants flowers in the yard. She even enjoys catering to him. Then something new comes along that looks fun and challenging and it's back to take-out.

with a Leo:

If these two can't keep romance alive, the rest of us may as well give up! A Leo man and an Aries woman are both romantics who not only believe in love but absolutely need it in their lives. Their love affair will have it all—passionate love, just as passionate fights, and tender reunions.

He isn't put off by a strong woman; in fact, he respects the way she needs to feel she's accomplishing something. He's that way, too. They are different enough to add spice to the relationship but similar enough to want basically the same things out of life.

They could get into a competing egos standoff, because both think *their* way is the right way, plus they both need someone to listen to them and give them attention. It could destroy their relationship, but she won't let it. She's smart enough to know that she has a basically good man who just needs a lot of appreciation and devotion, so she'll devise little ways to show him how important he is to her. Example: when she goes to the store she might ask him, "Is there something special I can pick up for you?" Even if there isn't, he'll love that she thought to ask.

Their love will change and mature over time and become less all-encompassing, but it will never wither and die for lack of enthusiasm. They could become the couple who celebrates many years together by getting re-married with all the trimmings.

If he sees her weaknesses and loves her anyway, she just may learn to love herself.

with a Virgo:

In her uninhibited way, an Aries woman plunges ahead with this romance, ignoring the little voice that whispers, "Be cautious." If a Virgo man came with instructions they would say, "Not suitable for excitement or flights of fancy." She always was too impatient to read the directions.

He is utterly captivated by her charms and hormones have clouded his usually astute judgment, so in the dating stage neither notices the clues that point to an enormous difference in personality styles. Hers is direct and unencumbered by second-guessing as in, "My mind is made up—don't confuse me with the facts." He's just the opposite . . . analytical and rational. He's uncomfortable with her more innovative ideas, and often thinks she isn't being sensible. If he tries to hold her back, her anger and irritation can poison the relationship. Of all women to correct or criticize, an Aries woman is the poorest choice. She doesn't take anyone's guff and, if someone picks on her, she throws it right back.

Money is an issue. He thinks she isn't responsible enough and she sees him as a penny-pincher who would rather put money in their IRA than spend a little to enhance their lives. True, she gets carried away with the credit cards, but makes up for it by cutting back somewhere else.

He's a workaholic who judges himself on how well he does his job. She can be, too, but she won't get ahead through grinding effort—she'll make sure she has fun along the way. This relationship won't last long without counseling of some sort, even if it's self-help.

with a Libra:

She prefers the honest approach—it saves so much time—but a Libra man hides his irritation and annoyance, even from himself, just to keep everyone happy and the atmosphere pleasant. This drives an Aries woman crazy; she likes a little fight now and then. She doesn't understand subtle hints or mysterious undercurrents . . . or people who live that way. She lays her cards face-up on the table, while he plays his close to the chest. Which one wins? He does, of course. But if winning means losing her, he might try to be more honest about his real feelings.

These are two self-confident and take-charge people who have different ways of handling a challenge. She jumps in and assumes everything will work out. He thinks and rethinks all aspects of the situation, until she wonders if he'll ever make a decision. He could use some of her certainty, while she could stand to be more cautious, like him. They could learn a lot from each other if they were so inclined, but they can't change their personalities, not even for love.

Her optimism and enthusiasm encourage him to take a chance and go for what he wants, and his sociability is perfect for a woman who likes to get out and about like she does. But this union will require self-awareness and communication—a dicey situation at best, with a Libra man. If they can work around their different natures, he will find that when she's secure and happy, she's a loyal partner in the truest sense of the word.

with a Scorpio:

It's not that an Aries woman cares about control the way a Scorpio man does, she just wants to have her own way. A Scorpio man is the last man to be dominated by anyone, especially a woman. She won't put up with shenanigans like his jealous rants, or worry about tiptoeing around his sensitive issues. She doesn't have the time or inclination to *baby* a man.

She knows good communication is vital between a man and a woman, but a Scorpio man is not a prospect for candor. He's offended when she tells him exactly what she thinks, but he keeps it inside. He's a private person and doesn't even want anyone to *know* him, let alone criticize him. She has to push him beyond his limits before he gets angry enough to fight back. He will win in his own way, because he never lets anyone get the best of him. For instance, he never refuses to do something she asks, he just doesn't do it. They can get into power struggles that aren't pretty.

If they have individual areas of responsibility and give each other plenty of room, they can accomplish a lot. When they are united, few, if any, will ever get the best of them. But if it isn't working, she won't hang on indefinitely, hoping things will improve. When they split, he will either act like she doesn't exist or hold a grudge against her forever.

with a Sagittarius:

These two believe they have found their respective soul mates when they meet—they get along that well. Like him, she wants what she wants and has the gumption to go after it, regardless of the consequences. They feed off each other's ideas and come up with adventures neither would think of alone. They will be the best of friends forever, unless they fall in love and take it to the next level. Then the Sagittarius man is not such a good match for an Aries woman. In the long run, she doesn't need more excitement—she needs someone to ground her and help her make practical decisions. And, unless he's at the stage in his life where he wants to settle down, their relationship will run into problems. Even an Aries woman eventually wants stability in her life so she can get ahead, build some security, and raise a family.

However, their similarities can keep them going because they understand each other's passions. His passions tend toward the active life and sports, and hers center on her career. They give each other space to go off and do their own thing, as long as the trust is there.

They love to laugh, they're generous with their friends and families, and they're always up for a good time—people are drawn to their high spirits and endless energy. They don't slow down unless one of them is sick, which isn't often, since both have incredible recuperative abilities.

If they're both ready to pledge loyalty to each other, this can be a successful relationship and, if enthusiasm equals success, chalk one up for love!

with a Capricorn:

Here's the problem: If she calls him at work and excitedly reports, "Honey, guess what? I just won two tickets to Las Vegas for this weekend!" he will have to determine first, if he wants to go, second, the possibility of losing money at the tables, and third, if he can afford to take time away from work. (He often works on the weekends.)

His ambition is amazing and his goal is no less than the top of the mountain. She's a tough competitor too, but can get sidetracked by something that looks like more fun or a bigger challenge. Besides, it's lonely at the top, isn't it?

An Aries woman and a Capricorn man can form a dynamic partnership—in business. Working together with their individual roles well-defined, they combine his deliberate, practical actions with her spontaneous, creative ones. But if they get married, he has certain expectations of what a wife should be and she won't change to suit anyone's expectations.

Their personalities can grate against each other. He's accustomed to making decisions and doing things in his own efficient way, but she isn't the type to play "little girl" to his "big daddy." Not since she was in her twenties has she acted as anyone other than her real self just to get along. She's always resented being a female in a male-dominated society anyway.

He could learn to be more spontaneous like her, and she could learn to be more organized like him. And pigs could fly, if they were crows and not pigs.

with an Aquarius:

She is mightily attracted to this interesting guy and she tries to take the lead in the romance, as usual, but when she looks back, he isn't following. There he goes, wandering down his own path—not hers. An Aquarius man is unpredictable, the very quality that attracted her but, at the same time, is hard for her to cope with. He fears a too-intimate relationship that encroaches on his independence. But she has a lot of love to give, and how can she give it when he keeps his distance?

An Aries woman isn't accustomed to changing her behavior to suit someone else, but she must stop pushing for the ideal relationship she dreamt of and let him be himself. It will take time to adjust to his on-again, off-again style. He doesn't necessarily want to stay single; he just needs the freedom to do things his own way. When she realizes there are lots of paths that love can take and no one right one, she's getting closer.

He likes to work with groups with a shared goal to improve the planet or bring new information in. She will tackle any goal she believes in. If they join forces, they can accomplish wonders with her vision and energy and his ideas and commitment. It might not be the easiest thing, but if they love each other enough, they can forge their own unique relationship that works for them both.

with a Pisces:

She finishes his sentences for him. An Aries woman has a hard time waiting while he searches for the right words. But a Pisces guy has so much going on in his head and sees things from so many perspectives, it takes time to assemble his thoughts. Then he begins to analyze how his words will be taken and, well, it just goes on and on. She likes people to be direct and to-the-point; anything else she considers a waste of valuable time.

A Pisces man lives in a different world than she, a world of feeling and depth and wonder, and sometimes confusion. He's had many jobs and has worn many hats, each of which he will eventually discard so he can try on another. He even changes his persona so there's really very little about him that seemingly endures.

Her habit of telling the blunt truth will hurt his feelings. He doesn't respond immediately. He thinks about it, chews it over, and thinks of other women who have similarly injured him as he slides into the familiar role of victim. It's just a matter of time before his subtle emotional pressure and sulky silences drive her to the brink. She's not good at mind games and is defenseless against indirect hostility.

On the off chance they *do* stay together, they will have an unconventional approach to marriage. Instead of sticking to traditional roles, they will divide their responsibilities according to which one is best suited for a particular job. She will take the lead because she's used to being the strong one and that's okay by him.

The Taurus Woman

April 20–May 20

A Taurus daughter is sweet and good-natured and has simple needs—to be loved and treated kindly, to be fed, to be safe, and to be in comfortable surroundings. As a youngster, she enjoyed nature and loved to plant a seed and watch it grow. These remain her priorities throughout her life, and as long as she has them, the sun is shining on her world.

At school, she was shy and quiet, preferring one or two best friends to a crowd. At home, she was mother's little helper and strived to do the right thing. She didn't like chores, but the reward of a kiss or a thank-you made it worthwhile. One day, she attacked a huge mess—probably her bedroom. She sorted, organized, and cleaned and didn't quit until it was done. She loved the feeling of accomplishment, and never again would she hesitate to take on a challenging task.

As a teen, she might have been sexual or conservative, but once she discovered how enjoyable sex was, her earthy nature took over and it became central to her life.

She had a great desire to love and nurture a child and wouldn't hesitate to adopt, if necessary. Her children became a most important part of her life.

When she fell in love, she knew it would be forever. Her expectation was a little house with pink roses growing on a white picket fence with a happy family inside. She loved nothing more than being at home with her loved ones.

If her mate was *not* kind and loving, she put up with it as long as she and her children had security. She carried on as usual and seldom confided in anyone about her unhappiness; in fact, she was the last one to realize it if the situation was impossible. It could take years. Knowing when to let go and make a change is her greatest challenge.

As she gets older, at least one long-term relationship has failed, so she plans to choose carefully and be certain before giving her heart again. But there are no guarantees. If she's hurt too many times, she may give up on marriage and remain single. She'll have love affairs, but make no commitments.

In maturity, she's less skeptical and more open to life's mysteries that can't be seen or touched. She can take a chance now and then, and knows she can't control everything. She even admits that her advice isn't always perfect.

She realizes a high-pressure life is hard on her nervous system, and she learns to take care of her body with regular exercise. She pampers herself with good food, a little chocolate, maybe a pot of tea or a glass of wine. She has realized that the love she sought so fervently was always within her.

The Taurus woman in love . . .

with an Aries:

When an attractive Aries man thrills a Taurus woman with his undivided attention, she's a goner. The sex is great and, for a while, they mistake the heady rush of chemistry for love—at least *she* does. When it diminishes enough so she can start thinking again, she begins to wonder.

First, he isn't happy unless he's busy. There is always somewhere to go. She enjoyed the excitement at first, and she thought things would settle down once they were a couple. But he's always thinking ahead, making plans. Maybe he'll take up sailing, perhaps try a different job, or possibly pursue a business venture he and his friends are thinking about. It's disconcerting to her because she doesn't like running around for the sake of being busy. When she's in love, she enjoys the comfort of a quiet evening at home with her lover, a good meal, maybe a video, popcorn, and later, fabulous sex. He'd rather have the sex first and then, oops, gotta run.

He doesn't realize what an asset she can be to him. If his ideas aren't practical, she'll gently talk him down. If his plan requires hard work to make it a reality, she'll happily work as long and as hard as it takes. She'll have to do a lot of tolerating and putting up with, and she's good at that.

His free-spirit adds fun and excitement to her life, but is hard on her sense of security. That doesn't mean she won't keep trying to make it work; it all depends on how fabulous the sex is.

with another Taurus:

Once upon a time, a Taurus woman had a Taurus boyfriend who lived in the adjoining town. He visited every weekend and they found all kinds of things to do. They washed their cars, cleaned out her garage, painted the living room, and worked on the yard. It was great at first; boy, did they get a lot done! But after a few months, she broke up with him: too boring even for her. A female Taurus is more interesting than a male Taurus because she has more creative energy.

Two Taurus Suns are compatible, but some of the sign's negative qualities will be emphasized. For instance, a relaxing evening at home is a wonderful thing, but not when that's the only entertainment. And it's great to know where you're going and what you want out of life, but to never let one's imagination soar or take a chance on pursuing a dream can deaden the spirit. It's better to have a partner who can provide a balance.

Overindulgence can be reinforced by both. Too many delicious meals and tasty snacks can put the weight on. Drinking too much is an obvious peril, as is overdoing drugs. Too much sex, well that's *not* bad, and it won't last long, anyway.

These two can get into a comfortable rut, but a rut all the same. If they don't find a way to add some light-hearted play or stimulating friends, one of them will eventually feel confined and want to get out.

Will they actually do it? They could stay together long past the time when they were enjoying their relationship. But who knows? Maybe that works for them, too.

with a Gemini:

These people reside in two different worlds. She lives in a down-to-earth world where you get what you pay for, and there's no such thing as a free lunch. He lives in his head where anything is possible and there's no limit of possibilities. To her, *change* means rearranging the living room. To him, it means a new job in a distant city. Variety is the spice that keeps life interesting for a Gemini man. What's appealing to him today might bore him to pieces tomorrow.

He believes talking about doing something is just as good as actually doing it . . . better, even. She believes actions speak louder than words, and that *doing* creates things, not thoughts. His failure to take action will mystify her at first and later, drive her nuts.

Being responsible and keeping your word is second nature to her and she thinks everyone should live by that code. She has a pot roast ready to eat at 6 o'clock, just as she told him she would, but he arrives home at 8:40 and "didn't have time to call" or "didn't realize what time it was." Maybe he *was* playing computer games online with his pals, but all night?

Grim as it may sound, it isn't all bad. She loves to listen to this interesting guy and hear about his travels, his different jobs, and his experiences. He helps her think outside the box of her orderly world and gives her a glimpse into one with countless possibilities. She is more than happy to give structure and stability to him, if it's possible to stabilize the wind.

with a Cancer:

When a Taurus woman is out and about, there is a little thought that is constantly in the back of her mind: "When will I get home?" No other sign in the Zodiac has this love of home . . . except a Cancer. To buy a house, fill it with the things they love, and know it is there to come home to is security.

Since they have similar likes and dislikes, they adjust fairly easily once they get settled, but if she is moving into *his* house, he might have a moment of panic when he sees how much stuff she has. It isn't easy for him to move his things over and create closet and drawer space. He saves everything with connections to his past, or that he has grown accustomed to, no matter how useless or obsolete. She loves her belongings, too, especially those that make her feel valued and secure in the love of family and friends. When hers joins his and they add theirs, they will have to rent a storage shed to handle the overflow.

Even though he's basically gentle, he does have a controlling side that can come as an unpleasant surprise to her. She resists being told what to do and when pressed, will resist all the harder. Her willfulness is an affront to him and a signal that his security is threatened. Rather than force the issue, he'll withdraw and let his silence speak for him.

This behavior irritates her to no end. Luckily, a Taurus woman is least likely to give up on him, even if he is an old Crab.

with a Leo:

Picture this: delectable food served with a fine wine and enjoyed by candlelight in beautiful surroundings. After the meal, mutual massages with soft music playing in the background. Do these folks understand the art of fine living, or what?

Granted, this cozy little scene is more likely when they are in the early stages of romance. Later on, it becomes too much trouble for some people, but not for her. A Taurus woman spares no effort to preserve her marriage and her sex life.

Both are creative souls. She has an artistic nature and loves to make something with her own hands. He's adept at some art form as well, and they both want something real to look at as a result of their efforts. They can encourage each other in their endeavors.

He admits she has good taste . . . after all, she chose him, didn't she? This is his slightly humorous way of reinforcing how lucky she is to have him and, of course, she agrees—she's no fool. If she didn't make him feel important and loved, he might find someone who will.

Of course, life will have its way with them and stress happens, so what about disagreements? They are both extremely stubborn, but they aren't likely to give up on their relationship, either, and will try everything to make it work. The end of the line will come for him if he no longer feels proud to have her as his mate. With her, a loveless marriage is heartbreaking, but starting over is unthinkable: she'll stick it out.

with a Virgo:

When a Virgo man sees a Taurus woman's filing cabinets (she labels and files everything, even her recipes, greeting cards, and old journals) something whispers to him, "This is the one."

These two know how to get things done! He always has a house or yard project for them and she works right beside him, delighted to have a man who doesn't watch sports all weekend. But too much of a good thing is still too much, and if they don't make time for leisure and fun, the spark can go out of the relationship.

One thing that's hard on her is how he consistently points out something she forgot to do, didn't finish, or didn't do correctly. A Taurus woman often doesn't recognize how talented and bright she is, so criticism is hard on her. But he's a perfectionist and is keenly aware of mistakes or imperfections, his own included, though he keeps those to himself! She wants to keep him happy, so she just keeps trying harder to please him, but beneath the surface, some of her love for him will have dimmed. Even so, her solid, conservative values blend well with his, and they understand each other.

This couple may not be known for their dazzling parties or scintillating conversation, but they're both willing to help someone build a deck or paint a house.

Unless he does something a lot worse than complain or work too much, she won't jump ship. They may even have the satisfaction of celebrating their golden wedding anniversary on one condition: he stays committed to her and their marriage.

with a Libra:

He's just throwing out random thoughts to hear how they sound, but she thinks he's serious. She runs to get paper and pen and make a to-do list. Silly Taurus! She hasn't yet learned that a Libra man loves to discuss ideas, but that doesn't mean he actually plans to carry them out! She's such a realist and so ready to do whatever it takes to make something happen. She's frustrated when he says, "Come over here and relax; you don't need to write this down." Foiled again!

He's thoughtful and shows up with little surprises that never fail to delight her, and she cherishes these little proofs of his love. He's one man who was born knowing how to make people feel good. She's happy, he's happy—everyone is happy, right? The problem here is obvious—they can't be happy all the time. This is still LIFE. But he sandbags his anger or discontent so he can keep the peace. She's slow to take offense and often ignores what she doesn't want to see, but when she *does* see a problem, she wants to get it out in the open so they can solve it. Talking about it is the *last* thing he wants to do! Eventually, every couple has to deal with their issues or see the resentments begin to add up.

She lets her own opinions be known and expects honesty from him—she can detect phoniness a mile away. If she notices that he is insincere with other people, she loses faith in his sincerity with her. This can be a serious problem since it affects the trust she has in him.

with a Scorpio:

Ah, the dreaded, "opposites attract" phenomenon! According to astrology lore, there is a powerful magnetic attraction between a Taurus and a Scorpio, but few long-lasting unions. They are both stubborn, but while he doesn't change for anyone or anything, she will often adapt to please him, not because she's a Taurus, but because she's a woman.

They both have a jealous streak, but she actually needs a reason, while he is jealous just because he's that way. If they stay together long enough, he will finally learn that she doesn't say things she doesn't mean and that she is completely loyal. Underlying his eventual trust is a mountain of accusations and detective work on his part.

Another difference: She's truthful and upfront and she expects no less from him. She needs to be aware that he will always have his secrets, and sometimes even a secret life, that she will never know about. It can take years for her to discover this.

It's extremely hard for a Taurus woman to understand the complex nature of a Scorpio man because she is simple, in the good sense of the word. If they were automobiles, she would be a little blue sedan and he would be a Humvee—preferably armored.

In the end, it feels like a test of endurance for her and to him, a test of wills. Nevertheless, Taurus and Scorpio share a strong bond that can, indeed, last. Separate residences can be the key. Or they can decide to keep the friendship and let the love relationship go.

with a Sagittarius:

A Sagittarian man put the "roam" in romance. He won't *always* be unfaithful, but it's no comfort to know The Donald has a Saj Moon. When a Taurus woman is in love, she's thinking forever, and he's thinking, well, he isn't really thinking about their relationship—he's waxing his skis, buying airplane tickets, or packing his duffle bag for the next adventure.

She likes to travel and have adventures, too, but not if it means being cold, uncomfortable, and miserable in a drafty tent or on a windswept mountain. She is the original "material girl," who likes to know she has her own soft sheets and fluffy towels nearby. To him, it's not what he owns, it's where he's been.

They have their moments when they're sitting by the fire, discussing life. He's an intelligent conversationalist and she's easygoing and cheerful. But their basic natures just don't mesh. For instance, he cannot make her hurry. The best he can do is to coax her along with humor. And she can't get him to stay home. He has itchy feet that must keep moving.

Because of his travels and the many people he meets, he can always find a job he likes better than the one he has, or at least that *sounds* better. Moving, especially far away, is not for her. She resists even moving to a different house.

She hates the bills that stack up when he's between jobs, but she puts up with it. If he's irresponsible with money, she should keep her finances separate as much as possible, enjoy his company while it lasts, and forget the "ever after" part.

with a Capricorn:

These two make a good team, as in, "Hitch up the team and let's get this field plowed." These two can fall into a routine and work from sun-up to sundown. Still, if they're happy doing that, well, the world needs workers, and at least they're on the same page.

So he is a little bossy; she's more of a follower and can let him take the lead, as long as his decisions make sense to her. At least with him, she knows what to expect and she likes that he's responsible with money. She feels safer with him than with most other signs and loves the assurance of knowing he's got her back.

It just gets better: their priorities include home and family and building security. He respects her for being astute in money matters, especially in real estate matters. Of course, couples can always fight about money, but at least they have the same value system. She may spend money more freely than he does, but he appreciates the fact that her biggest expenditures are for their home. As long as she buys quality, and it was on sale, he won't complain too much.

Watching their portfolio grow will thrill them right down to their practical little toes. Others may scoff at these two worker-bees, but, eventually, they'll have the last laugh. As time passes, it turns out that security *is* more important than exhilarating love, regardless of how grand it is.

with an Aquarius:

Just when a Taurus woman falls in love with an Aquarius man, he pops in and says he is moving to Australia and is that okay with her? Or he is selling the business and is going to take up ceramics . . . in New Mexico! These little vignettes illustrate the Aquarian man's habit of periodically shaking off routine and changing direction—it's the only way he knows to live. To a Taurus woman, a total change of plans can come like a bolt of lightning, putting a crack in her serene world. And yet, she can't help but be attracted to him.

He's different from anyone she's ever known and that's what made him interesting. But she has to know what to expect in life, and with him, she never will. He has dreams. He dreams of what might be and of how he can change the world, at least his little corner of it. She's down-to-earth and practical: she has dreams too, but first she wants to get the bills paid off.

He's a joiner, and whatever group he supports is going to take a lot of his free time. He needs freedom to attend meetings or do *whatever* with friends, which is unsettling to her. She can't let him go and not wonder if he's with another woman.

She will have to give up something to live with this guy, and that *something* may be the very security she longs for. If she's working and he's not, it drives her nuts. In time, he may settle down and his family become more important, but is she patient enough to wait?

with a Pisces:

These two have a lot in common. She has a shy side and so does he. She is undemanding and so is he. They understand each other, or at least she *thinks* they do. This is one of the Taurus woman's best signs, if all goes well.

He is a supporter, a protector, and a generous lover. In fact, he is just about everything she wants in a man. They can talk for hours about their religious or spiritual beliefs, their goals in life, and their hopes for the future.

He seems strong and confident at first, and for as long as there are no big problems. But when important decisions or difficult situations arise, she may find out he's less than confident; in fact, he is often un-sure and expects her to give him direction. This frustrates and confuses her because she thought she knew him.

In his world, everything is always shifting and changing. He was happy yesterday, now what's wrong? She's at a loss to understand his sulky silences. Is it that she didn't show enough enthusiasm about his new project? Maybe she wasn't demonstrative enough? It's just like a Taurus woman to think it's all her fault. He doesn't share his feelings because even he isn't sure what they are. They come from a place deep inside where the painful memories live.

He plays havoc with her sense of security and she detests finding out something that she should have known all along. She'll confront him on it, but if she pressures him, he may just glide away to become one more page in her book of memories.

THE GEMINI WOMAN
MAY 21–JUNE 21

A Gemini girl might have kept her parents on their toes, but at least they never had to worry that she didn't have any friends. She befriended a variety of people, younger, older—it didn't matter—she liked them all. She often picked out the child who was different in some way because her curiosity was triggered.

She showed the other kids how to play a game or organized them in an activity. She was funny and well-liked, although not especially sympathetic. She got good grades, even though all her homework wasn't handed in. She could grasp concepts quickly if she applied herself, which she often didn't.

She was a tomboy who wasn't big on playing with dolls. If she did play house, she always got to say who played which role.

As a young woman she had a lot of boyfriends, but none for long. She got bored and looked around for someone new, not because she was shallow, but because she really believed she would find her perfect mate. She had a feeling someone was out there who could make her complete and take away her loneliness.

She probably married young because it was another frontier to explore. Or perhaps she forgot to take a pill and got pregnant. She often marries more than once. It's that old dream of finding her soul mate that keeps her trying.

What she could use is a man who is more practical than she is and knows important stuff, like that the phone is getting turned off on Tuesday. You'd think she'd protect this lifeline to the outside world, but alas, she forgot to pay the bill, if she even opened the envelope. She knows she can be an "airhead," and would laugh if someone called her "Most Likely to Leave the Baby on the Bus."

She is never boring and can talk about any number of topics as long as she isn't pressed for details and accuracy. Men are attracted to her wisecracking ways and funny stories.

A Gemini woman adapts to the role of parent easier than a Gemini man. She does crafts with her kids and then dashes off to take her turn driving a neighborhood group to a baseball game or ballet. She can be a stay-at-home mom as long as she can go to the mall, take a class, or call one of her two dozen friends—you know, stay busy not bored.

As she gets older, she becomes more honest with herself, and more forgiving of herself and others. She learns to value the enduring friendships she has built. She discovers self-discipline through her career, and learns to get the bills paid on time, usually. She discovers she can create the excitement and novelty she needs in her life without looking for a man to supply it. And, most important, she learns that her other half, her twin soul, is within.

The Gemini woman in love . . .

with an Aries:

A Gemini woman doesn't appreciate unsolicited advice or, worse yet, being told what to do, so when an Aries man does that very thing, he'll soon learn it doesn't work with her. She's a moving target, however, and won't hang around if he's too bossy or hard to get along with.

While there may be fireworks, at least there's a spark, and this is someone who won't bore her to tears. He's attracted to her as well, because she's a fascinating lady and keeps him guessing. They're both full of life and their active minds keep them up until the wee hours, talking about everything under the sun.

After the first thrill of romance has worn off, he isn't as good company. If the conversation veers off into a subject that doesn't affect him directly, he loses interest; he might even tune her out. She doesn't take it personally and can usually fill in the emotional gaps with her friends and family. It's just one of the little ways she will have to adjust, but as Lily Tomlin said in the 1980s classic *Nine to Five*, "I'm a tree, I can bend."

His high energy level is the main attraction for her. A man has to be interesting or a relationship isn't worth the trouble. They can get along pretty well once he realizes she's intelligent enough to make her own decisions and lets up on the demands.

with a Taurus:

Life suddenly gets a lot more complicated for a Taurus man when he falls for a Gemini woman. She's a high-speed connection for him and he isn't sure he has the bandwidth to handle it. Nor does he feel 100 percent comfortable with her friends. But if anyone can talk him into doing something different, it's her!

Her low tolerance for boredom is behind the creative ideas she comes up with. She'll find out soon enough that he doesn't even like to take in an unplanned movie, let alone a spontaneous trip or party. At first he'll do it for love and make the effort. Later, when the relationship gets more comfortable, he'll begin to resist. She'll try to stir things up, maybe by making him jealous. That really doesn't sit well with him and they might end up in a whole new fight.

For these two to get along, they may have to consider separating on a regular basis to do their individual things. Then he has his peaceful time to recharge, and she can enjoy the give-and-take of a lively argument with someone else, an event he won't mind missing.

She may be the best thing that ever happened to him, and when it's over, he'll never forget her. How can he, when some of her stuff is still hanging around his apartment long after she's moved out? But not to worry. He will have everything neatly boxed up and labeled when, or if, she ever comes back for it.

with another Gemini:

Two twins? Let's see—that makes four of them! Could get interesting, especially when they are both so good at saying what the other person wants to hear, and then going their own way. Talk about your intricate mind games!

They are both communicators, but she likes to talk about what happened today, who called and what was said. He focuses more on subjects like sports, politics, or how things work, seldom on conversations. Still, there's no denying there's a bond here. They both love long talks that go on into the night, and fragmented conversations that only they understand. They don't even have to see each other in person: the telephone is their lifeline—or email or instant messaging, all of which are Gemini-like inventions. They also love movies, books, friends, classes, and social activities. In fact, these two have so much in common, they sometimes make better friends than lovers.

They are both quick-witted and sharp-tongued. The occasional hurtful remark may slip out, but on the whole, they enjoy spirited debates and intellectual sparring.

If one of them gets bored and uses flirting as a diversion, this twosome can blow up quickly.

Nervous tension and debt can build up when neither is inclined to take care of business, but they've made a good start as friends. Off they go in their convertible, with their matching iPods and laptops. Who's to say they can't make a go of it?

with a Cancer:

OK, so she isn't Miss Sensitive, but her heart's in the right place. A Cancer man who loves a Gemini woman is going to have to either settle for that or be consistently offended. Even if she's totally devoted to him, she isn't able to censor her every offhand comment to see if it passes his sensitivity test. Their relationship will succeed or fail depending on how much *he* wants it, because she can't change her personality.

He falls in love with her spunk and sense of humor, and the way she spends all her free time with him. It's when she gets bored playing domestic goddess that things take a downward turn. Maybe she signs up for a night class without consulting him, or worse yet, takes a job that requires travel. The Cancer man's life is built on his emotional needs, and he can't tolerate a mate who isn't around.

He will never understand her need for novelty and change. Her many friends of both sexes, her flirtatiousness, her independence—these things threaten his security. Even her inclination to move frequently can conflict with his desire to put down permanent roots.

If they have children, she will settle down some, but this stay-at-home mom won't stay at home. She'll pile the kids in the car and off they'll go.

This is a strange combination that won't last unless both are consciously aware of their different emotional needs and have good communication (is that even possible with a Crab?) She must ask herself: "Do I always want to be on guard not to offend, instead of being my natural, witty, smart-alecky self?" Nah.

with a Leo:

In spite of her independent nature, a Gemini woman can become devoted to one man. She can, that is, if that man recognizes her need for a variety of interesting friends and experiences. Luckily, a Leo man loves to have fun and enjoy life as much as she does. He falls for her quick wit and interesting personality.

But his is an ultra-sensitive sign, ego-wise. He loves her sense of humor, as long she doesn't make fun of him, even in jest. She also needs to watch her natural habit of interrupting people because, if she does, he'll take it as a sign of disrespect, something he can't tolerate.

She likes a lot of attention and he does, too, so they will have to indulge each other by being thoughtful and giving credit where credit's due. He can make her happy with short, unexpected trips to new places, taking her out where she can meet people, and remembering that, for her, good talk is as important as good sex.

Here are ways she can please him if she hasn't tired of him yet, and after all, a Leo man *is* a great catch. She can solicit his opinion, ask him to order for her at a restaurant, and devise new ways of praising him without sounding phony. If anyone can do it, she can.

with a Virgo:

They must have met at work; how else could they have found time to get to know each other? He's notorious for being a workaholic; she's famous for being over-committed and running around at breakneck speed. If they slow down long enough to have sex, they're doing well.

Here's a guy as smart as she is, and he just might help her on her career path. He can talk about work forever, and his feedback is invaluable. So far, so good, but trouble lurks when they try to co-habit.

A Virgo man is a clean freak. A dirty sock under the sofa or an unmade bed and he can't think straight. A Gemini gal likes a clean house, too, but she has a busy life; meetings, a part-time job, possibly a lunch date with her old boss. Can a Virgo stand to have all the stuff of her busy life strewn around? Can she stand to listen to him complain about it?

Another thing: a Gemini woman hates to be criticized. Either she already knows her faults or she isn't going to, so his critical comments just annoy her. There are other tricky areas in their relationship. He's more practical than she is, all the more for him to criticize. But she's more willing to try something new than he is, all the more likely she gets bored. Here's their saving grace: if they rarely see each other, there's little time to fight.

with a Libra:

It's hard to imagine a Libra man and a Gemini woman spending a quiet evening at home: it must happen, but it just isn't them. Never was a couple so well-suited for the social circuit. They love to get out and see people—and be seen. They have scads of friends and are known for their parties, although the food may be take-out or catered; she isn't one to cook. They attend all sorts of events including sports, culture, politics, and music, and everything in between.

Their relationship can be ruined because of one thing: lack of communication. Although they both talk a good game, they don't always play the honesty card. For example: He's always well-turned-out and attracts female attention. If there's an attractive brunette hanging on him all night, the Gemini girl will drum up a little action of her own to make him jealous. If he gets jealous, he'll find subtle ways of letting her know or getting even. It's doubtful he'll tell her outright. These little games can nibble away at their happiness until it disappears like a piece of cheese on a mousetrap.

A Libra man, with his insincere but winsome ways, doesn't let on when he's angry. A Gemini woman, with her quick, sarcastic tongue, says what pops into her mind. So it seems like most of their arguments are started by her. But he is seldom innocent, just quieter about it.

However, they both are good at ignoring things and forgetting about them. Some things *are* better left unsaid and unfought over.

with a Scorpio:

So what if she's a natural-born flirt and he's a suspicious jealousy freak? So what if she's ready to go on a moment's notice, and he's not into spontaneity? So what if she has a low tolerance for people who don't communicate, and he's the silent type? At first, they aren't aware of their differences except for the only one that matters—their sexes. There are many others, and they will have to be addressed sooner or later.

The Scorpio man is passionate about certain things, including his favorite football team and his vintage auto. In a relationship, he can be detached if he isn't totally involved—or consumed by love and incredibly possessive if he is. When he's jealous of her co-workers, she knows she doesn't deserve it and it just makes her angry.

She could consider the tried-and-true ways couples mend their relationships: counseling (he won't go), discussion (already ruled that out), compromise (not his bag), separate residences (you're getting warmer), or giving up and learning to fight fair (he'll still have to win). If it seems hopeless, well, at least it was good while it was good, and that's about all we can expect when people with major personality differences get together.

Possibly the most dangerous part is this: she wants to be the one who ends things, but a Scorpio man is not the type to take rejection lightly. This could be a memorable romp—and an even more memorable break-up.

with a Sagittarius:

Before you can say "The mortgage payment's due," these two are off to Alaska to kayak and watch grizzly bears catch salmon. Her ideas spark his sense of adventure and the fun they have makes up for many minor disagreements along the way.

These two can chat for hours. She needs stimulation for her lively mind and he is always ready to explore something new or expound on his favorite theories. She's interested in his ideas in an intellectual way, but she doesn't get as emotionally involved as he does; nevertheless, she's with him in mind, if not in heart.

Although she's a worrier, she doesn't like to be. He looks on the bright side of life and he keeps her spirits up. He's an optimist who doesn't believe in conservatism. Everything about him is big, his dreams, his appetite, and his generosity, to mention a few. She will have to tolerate his over-spending and willingness to lend money to any of his innumerable friends.

They could adapt quite nicely to a transient lifestyle, or they may become perpetual students, indulging their innate curiosities about everything from Atlantis to Zanzibar.

One thing a Gemini woman hates is being bored, something she won't have to worry about with him. However, at a certain time in her life, when she has children, for instance, she needs some stability. That's when his hell-bent-for-leather attitude begins to wear on her and she'll wish he could be content to settle for a weekly paycheck and enough routine to keep the kids secure. How this works out is up to him.

with a Capricorn:

When a Capricorn man talks about the fun he had organizing his home office, a Gemini woman should follow her instinct and run like the wind! It's hard to visualize these two understanding each other. Their pacing is different and so are their interests. He likes to dig in and get to the bottom of things, say, the bills. The only thing she wants to dig into is her purse to get out her credit card!

He's serious, she's whimsical. He likes getting ahead, building for the future, and securing the comfortable life. She likes expressing herself, tak-

ing short trips, and tossing around ideas just for fun. He wants the traditional real Christmas tree and she prefers one that pops out of a box.

A Gemini woman, however, does have an inner desire for respecta-
bility, and so there are certain things she appreciates about a Capricorn
man: his stock portfolio, for instance. But she's never going to accept
limitations to her freedom and independence.

There are times, however, when she can become totally involved in
a project. When she does, she'll surprise even herself with her dedication. Then she can be as much of a workaholic as he is. Remember,
she is a Twin; he gets two people for the price of one! Instead of re-
joicing in his luck, however, he feels confused and queasy. He likes to
know exactly who he's married to—how quaint!

Their success as a couple comes down to commitment and tolerance, and keeping a marriage counselor on retainer.

with an Aquarius:

They'll start as friends and end as friends. That's not to say marriage
isn't a possibility, but they both regard being close friends as the necessary first step. When they get together, they both enjoy having a whole
new set of friends to meet, compare, and gossip about.

She respects his intellect and finds him *so* interesting to talk to,
while he likes her sense of humor and the way she can listen to him
talk about his adventures for hours.

They get along so well, in fact, that she may start to believe she's
found her perfect mate, after all.

Each has found, in the other, someone willing to give them the
breathing room they need, without feeling threatened. Neither is emotionally complicated. They both prefer to be somewhat detached and
free, not fanatically joined at the hip.

In time, she will expect them to proceed to the commitment level
(that would be her saner, more stable twin), and that's when she realizes things may not be as easy as they initially appeared. He wasn't
looking to settle down, he was just enjoying her company, mind, and
body. The test comes when she hands him the inevitable ultimatum. If
he actually commits, he passes. And if he marries her, she will know he

really and truly loves her, because ties that bind are not his thing. She should be proud.

with a Pisces:

Like Forrest Gump's box of chocolates, you never know what you're gonna get with a Pisces man. He could be an artist, musician, or bull-rider, but he uses his intuition and feeling nature to make decisions. His thought processes are uniquely his own and getting him to state his opinion firmly is like grabbing a fish out of the pond with your bare hands—it seldom happens. She gets impatient with him and throws out a flippant comment that affects him more than she realizes.

They are drawn to the same interests and share their music and books. They love going to a movie or having people over. As friends, they're great together, but when they establish their own household, the demands of daily living intrude to strike a discordant note to their harmonious love affair. Bills don't get paid and neither wants to make the hard decisions. Each is hoping the other will be the practical one and take care of business.

Neither needs to be the boss nor has a strong need to achieve or collect material possessions. It takes a Pisces man a while to decide what career to go for and a Gemini woman isn't exactly focused on her goals either, at least at first.

He has spiritual leanings and delves deeply into esoteric ideas. She reads a lot and wants to know about everything, but she doesn't go deeply into subjects, preferring to know a little about a lot of interesting things.

As time passes, they can learn to manage their affairs, though they'll never get a prize for consistency. Their life can take many directions and both will be surprised to see how it all turns out.

THE CANCER WOMAN
JUNE 22–JULY 22

A little Cancer girl is so sweet you want to hug her, but don't do it unless you know her well or she'll hide behind her mother's leg and give you a glare that says, "Leave me alone. I don't know you." Throughout her life, she'll be careful with her affections.

She's a child who needs a nightlight in her room for reassurance. She has other fears no one knows about because she doesn't talk about them.

She needs a ton of love and encouragement from her parents. She has a deep love for her family, and if she's lucky enough to have a loving mother, she is unusually attached to her. If not, or if they are estranged, it colors her personality for the rest of her life and makes it harder for her to love herself and others.

She adores animals and will gently care for a tiny baby bird or pick up a stray kitten and take it home to feed. Her desire to protect and nurture any helpless creature is one of her main traits, and she blossoms with a pet of her own to love.

She is tougher than she seems. Underneath her quiet and unassuming ways lie a strong will and independent nature. She is her own little person who knows what she wants. With her friends she's a leader, but only if she feels comfortable and secure in the situation.

She has at least one collection of something when she's small, and will collect other things as she goes through life. She's a natural saver, especially of anything with sentimental value like her old dolls and toys.

As a young woman, she wasn't openly flirtatious but sent subtle signals and waited for the guy to pick up on them and pursue her. She wanted a home of her own and married young. If misunderstandings and unhappiness ruined the marriage, she withdrew and closed off emotionally, but for years she obstinately held on, hesitant to make the final break.

For a Cancer woman, wounds cut deeply and heal slowly, so she is still harboring injustices and injuries from the past. She may remarry, but she still clings to whatever is dear to her—her children, a family home, or her cherished possessions. It's still hard to let go of anyone she loves— a grown child, for instance—but she's getting better at it. She knows, at least intellectually, that clinging and worry don't remove risks; they just create fear and illness.

As a mature woman, she's learned to be more honest about her relationships. She realizes that her insecurities and fears have been a big part of her problems. She's learning to live without trying to control everything.

She can now sometimes openly express her wants and needs to her husband or others instead of letting them try to guess—and guess wrong. Being straightforward isn't easy and holding back is still second nature, but she's making progress. Same with learning to love herself and her body . . . she's working on it.

The Cancer woman in love . . .

with an Aries:

Pairing the most insensitive male sign with the most sensitive female sign seems like a chump bet. It is. On the other hand, a Cancer woman loses respect for a man who can't stand his ground, so at least that's one barrier down, many more to go.

She's an old-fashioned girl who knows how to flutter an eyelash with the best of them, but underneath her modest facade is a wholesome sexuality just waiting to be unleashed in the right circumstances. Enter the Aries man with his take-charge attitude and masculine physique. No wonder it's love at first sight.

It's not his fault that he thinks he's going to be the boss in this relationship because she gives the impression of being passive and easily controlled. The *impression*, that is. In actuality, she's firmly planted in her own convictions, even though the quiet way she goes about it is deceiving. With a dominant Aries man, however, it may be hard for her to assert herself and maintain her self-confidence. If he ever blows up at her, she'll withdraw, thus spelling the end of any rapport between them.

What you see is what you get with an Aries man, just the opposite of her. He will never understand the deep emotions that lurk beneath her calm exterior. Logically, one could infer that this would be a better union for a brief, exhilarating affair than for a sustained, intimate partnership. One would be right.

with a Taurus:
It takes a while to get to know a Cancer woman, and a Taurus man has the patience to let things develop slowly. He doesn't pressure her; he just waits until she's ready to take the next step. When they finally get going, they discover their instincts were right and they turn out to be a pretty darn happy couple.

Contrary to popular belief, Cancer is not just the homebody type. She gets that reputation because she loves home and family. If she's a boss, she treats her employees like a big family and takes care of them. If she's dedicated to a career or other consuming interest, their relationship will be more challenging because she won't always be able to predict her schedule. However, he is generally tolerant, so they can work it out.

Any woman who likes to cook wants to do it for someone who appreciates it, and he's her guy. He doesn't enjoy eating in restaurants because they lack the homey atmosphere where he feels comfortable.

Good food is another nice connection they have as long as she doesn't try to get all *gourmet* on him.

A Taurus man doesn't understand the deep emotions of a Cancer woman, but it isn't necessarily a problem. Since so few people ever have, she's used to handling her inner life alone and prefers that he doesn't pry or try to understand. He doesn't like problems he can't fix, so they will probably both learn to take this in stride. All things considered, this is a pretty good match.

with a Gemini:

A motor home is perfect for a footloose Gemini man and a home-loving Cancer woman. If they have to wait for retirement before they can hit the road, what will their lives be like until then (assuming they make it that long)?

When they first get interested in each other, she wants to know if he has had financial troubles in the past. She always has one eye on her security and she keeps the other one on him. She needs to know that he loves her now and forever.

He has a lot of friends, business associates, and acquaintances to keep in touch with and he isn't above flirting a little just for fun. This raises havoc with her sense of security—how can she have peace of mind when he's always running off here or there with God knows who? Unless they have unusually good communication, she will withdraw and use manipulation and guilt to try to control him.

It's a fact that men in general don't like to talk about feelings, but a Gemini man takes that mind-set to the next level. He lives in his head, not his heart, and he doesn't even want to visit that country. If he fails to communicate or even listen when she needs to talk, she will be deeply hurt and duck under that Crab shell of hers. If they do have a talk, he'll discuss things in his rational, analytical way and, unless she knows that he really cares, she won't dredge up her feelings just for the sake of conversation. Bottom line for this couple? Not a good bet.

with another Cancer:

It might take some heavy-duty matchmaking to get two Cancer people together. They are inclined to be cautious for fear of rejection. Secrecy is another tendency they share, but as trust grows, so does openness. If they do fall in love, marriage will be the only thing that satisfies them.

It's a safe bet they will be involved in some cause for assisting the vulnerable. They might support an animal "no kill" society, work for legislation that protects children, capture feral cats and have them neutered or spayed, or offer their services in other ways to protect the helpless. This can be a bond that unites them even if other parts of their relationship aren't working so well.

These two will want children or may already have them. If theirs is a blended family, the stress of adapting to stepchildren and working out complicated relationships will be a huge challenge, but they will be committed to creating a stable home.

There's no end of things they can enjoy together: collecting things, redecorating the house, gardening, family photo albums and photography, cooking, even staying up late and sleeping in.

Problems? That they will both get in a mood at the same time and retreat to their respective shells, that they will try to get their needs met indirectly through manipulation, that they put so much of their efforts into home, work, and philanthropy they don't keep their sex life vibrant. Overall, there's a lot to recommend two Crabs in matching shells.

with a Leo:

If she's a gourmet cook, a Leo man will happily shop for the groceries. He'll love inviting friends over for good food and conversation, and to show off his talented and charming wife.

But, as Shakespeare said, here's the rub—their personalities are quite different. She's just as cautious as he is optimistic. She likes to keep the budget and handle the money, but a Leo man is not one to be kept on a financial leash. He will make decisions, regardless. If he puts money into a risky investment, she'll be a frazzled nerve ending. If he goes out and buys a plasma TV for the great room when they need another car, she'll show her displeasure in subtle but effective ways.

He's a high-spirited guy who likes to play and tease, but if he isn't careful he can hurt her feelings and the worst part is she won't let on. It's like her to withdraw instead of fight back.

In the best of Cancer/Leo relationships, he will shelter her from the harsh world and she will wait on him and make him feel like a king. That isn't to say she won't have a career of her own, but she will still baby him, pamper him, and cater to him because it's in her nature to take care of her loved ones.

If he's an arrogant, demanding-type Leo, she will suffer in silence and retreat into her shell. And being the great escape artist she is, he will find that one day she just silently skedaddled away.

with a Virgo:

A hard worker who brings home a steady paycheck is just the kind of man a Cancer woman admires. With a Virgo, she will have the security of knowing he'll never be without a job and he won't depend on her for support. Neither of them squanders money, so they can watch their nest egg grow with satisfaction, barring any surprises on Wall Street.

She loves to collect things—anything from antique jewelry or Fiesta Glass to ceramic pigs or postcards—so she's always looking for a place to display them. He's a handy guy with a hammer who will build shelves or even remodel the family room to give her a place to show off her treasures. That's just one way these two will go about creating a cozy home they can both enjoy.

Hopefully, she won't let his little criticisms hurt her because he can be a perfectionist. But if she feels secure in his love, she will learn to mentally switch him off when he's critical. He won't be as emotionally warm or giving as she would like, and he might write off her occasional moods as irrational and silly. But they both know life is never perfect and, unless there are other, serious problems, these are just irritations they can learn to tolerate. One way would be to allow each other some private time when they can each retreat and enjoy some needed solitude.

If they want children they'll be able to provide a happy home for them with a secure future. They have a better chance than most to have a rewarding, long-lasting relationship if nothing goes terribly awry.

with a Libra:

He doesn't have to *understand* her moods, just live with them, and a Libra man is good at ignoring anything he doesn't like. He'll learn to leave her alone when she needs privacy and not make a big deal about it or ask her to explain.

She wants everything to run smoothly and harmoniously, and so does he. These two can create a lovely home together that, to others, appears near perfect. But since neither of them wants to muddy the marital waters with anything unpleasant, they can get into the habit of stuffing their anger and not talking about their problems. In time, this leads to big-time resentments that can eventually destroy their love.

She is a giver, but if she doesn't trust completely, and she seldom does, she can withhold her affection to protect herself. He is more of a thinking type and likes to keep the conversation breezy and bright. These two aren't really on the same wavelength, so they'll have to work at it, perhaps with a counselor. If they can possibly find a way to communicate *some* of the time, they have a chance.

If that doesn't happen, she'll withdraw and give up on the relationship. She won't just decide one day to end it, though, and neither will he. They'll just continue on, living their own lives under the same roof, co-habiting and cooperating, but not in a loving way. The interesting thing is, they will continue to pretend everything is peachy-keen. No one will know it's over until it's over.

with a Scorpio:

A Cancer woman has a sixth sense that picks up vibrations from people. When she gets close to the right Scorpio man, she gets an unmistakable signal: here is someone she wants to know better. As their relationship progresses, their feelings run deep. They might never put it into words, but both know there is a powerful bond between them.

She feels she has finally found a man who understands her, although she has to teach him a few things before he actually does.

1. Even though he wants her all to himself, he can't interfere with her relationships with her women friends. She will never give them up to please him and doesn't feel she should have to.

2. There are times when she needs privacy to meditate, write in her journal, or just gaze at the moon. He has to let her have her private time without taking it personally or thinking she is shutting him out.

3. He must be 100 percent loyal and true. Luckily, in spite of his reputation, a Scorpio man doesn't much like casual sex. That doesn't mean he won't occasionally stray, but in his heart, he's loyal. It's a Scorpio thing.

His list would look like this: (1) Be honest. (2) Be true. (3) Be faithful. He only really cares about that one thing. Anything else, he can deal with.

He protects himself by never letting anyone really know him. She protects herself by withholding her love if she's hurt. Since destructive conflicts must be healed at a deep level of feelings, and neither of them is willing to share their pain, it's difficult to solve problems. They're not necessarily happy just because no one hears them fighting.

with a Sagittarius:
Here is a man who won't make her choose between him and her dog and, after all, that is her most important criteria in a relationship.

A Cancer woman is usually cautious, but there are times when she lets go of her fears and embraces her dreams—like when she meets a flamboyant Sagittarian who invites her to hop on the back of his cycle for a trip across country. She goes because it sounds exciting and because she feels something for him and wants to get closer. He wants to see new places and have an adventure. The relationship continues in this mode with him either ignoring or dismissing her feelings and her keeping her longing and anxiety to herself.

It doesn't help when he's too honest and blurts things out that hurt her feelings. He can be quite unaware of how his words come across to others. Again, his cavalier attitude blocks the closeness she needs to feel secure.

She craves a secure home base and family life, whether there are children or not. She doesn't want to move to another state or even another neighborhood. His goals and dreams can't be lived out in one place, no matter how inviting it is to visit.

However, a Cancer woman has noticed that she never gets exactly what she wants, and if she loves him, she won't break up with him just because he insists on his own independent interests. She will hang on to a relationship that isn't perfect. She lives her own inner life while she waits and hopes for a happy ending.

with a Capricorn:

These two represent the ideal parenting formula—love and discipline. A Cancer woman showers her children with unconditional love. A Capricorn man believes in firm discipline to raise well-behaved kids and good citizens. Both value their secure home and family life and this common bond will keep them together through the hard times.

She wants security above all and that includes a little home, however humble, and, of course, her children and beloved pets. A devoted and loyal partner is next, and everything else places further down the list.

A Capricorn man values security, too, but his basic drive is to work as long and as hard as it takes to reach the top of his career.

Both of them want to be the one to handle the money, but this and other things can be negotiated because they both have the same end in mind—their security. They go together to see their financial counselor and they make decisions based on sound advice.

If she lets him, he will be the traditional husband and she, the homemaker who takes care of all the details that make life run smoothly. It's almost hard to believe that these two are opposites in many ways and yet they are.

His occasional selfishness and preoccupation with work are hard on her. He doesn't understand how much she needs to feel he loves her deeply. This couple will stay together, but may eventually drift apart emotionally and each live separate inner lives. Their friends and even their children will think they have the perfect marriage.

with an Aquarius:

The first thing that draws a Cancer woman to an Aquarian man is how comical he is. He keeps her laughing with his offbeat humor and the unusual way he looks at life. She has a distinctive laugh that tickles him and a dry wit to match his.

His first inkling of trouble comes when he is going somewhere and she wants to know when he'll be back. "Oh no," he thinks, "she wants me on a timetable." He hates to feel pinned down. This is the sign least likely to give her what she needs to feel secure, so with him, she never will. He resists any pressure to settle down, or even to express deep feelings of love. Leery of sentiment, he prefers to keep some emotional distance, even in a one-on-one relationship. Neither is wrong; they're just different in their needs and outlook. A brief but fun romance fits them better than trying to build a life together.

Still in the first throes of love, however, she enjoys introducing him to her friends because he's such a character. They will have some good times, but if they marry, she has some adjusting to do, because he won't. Every time he changes jobs, her sense of security suffers. If he changes his interests or beliefs, which he is prone to do, it confuses her and again, she feels insecure.

Even his friends, who were at first fun and interesting, become an irritant sooner or later. She gets weary of always having someone around when she wants time alone with him. This is another case of her missing the emotional closeness that she desires but doesn't know how to create.

with a Pisces:

A Cancer woman and a Pisces man are both looking for a safe harbor. Can they find it in one another? They are both gentle souls who enjoy romantic movies and cry in the sad parts. He needs to feel understood more than anything else, and she is there for him—they have a calming influence on each other.

He's the underdog in some ways, which brings out her protective nature. She might wonder whether her feelings for him have more to do with compassion than love.

These two have a nonverbal communication and pick up each other's thoughts. But nonverbal messages can be misunderstood and don't take the place of good old-fashioned conversation. A Pisces man, especially, isn't aware how some of his invisible beliefs might control their lives. For instance, they may have too much debt, but he subconsciously fears that if they get all the bills paid off, she might leave him. These feelings are hard to uncover and lead to all kinds of misunderstandings.

She has psychic abilities which he understands. They can pursue these interests together and help each other develop their spirituality in a positive way.

As friends, they will always be there for each other. But marriage requires solving problems and dealing with difficult situations. If she always has to be the strong one, she might resent him for the very thing that drew her to him—his vulnerability. With neither willing to be direct and open about their feelings and differences, they won't fight, but neither will they be close.

The Leo Woman

July 23–August 22

A young Leo is the star in her household and the rest of the family knows it. Although she's a happy, delightful child who radiates an inner glow, she can be a handful at times. If told to do something, she thinks, "Why should they tell me what to do? Why can't I do what I want?" She has to be taught that someone else makes the decisions.

She has a box overflowing with fluffy net skirts, feather boas, glittery dresses, and jeweled tiaras so she can transform herself into the princess she knows she is. She loves to put on plays, especially with younger children so she can sweetly, but firmly, lead them through their proper roles with herself as the main character. She's kind to them, but she loves the feeling of being bigger, smarter, wiser, and more grown up.

In school, she's a good student who seeks recognition for her clever, lovely self and her accomplishments. All she wants is teacher approval, lots of friends, and to be loved and adored by peers and staff alike.

Not surprisingly, the Leo teenager loves movie stars and glamour. Monitoring the appropriateness of her clothing is an unending job for mom. When adolescent hormones erupt, the young Leo girl becomes a drama queen. Everything is either glorious or dreadful. Every teenage crush has a life and death quality as if her whole existence depended on one boy's approval.

She's not above stealing another girl's boyfriend. She doesn't know it yet, but she's going for reassurance of her self-worth as well as a feeling of superiority. She has yet to learn what's fair in love. She might like the most popular boy or the football star just for the ego-gratification, a cover for her own self-doubt.

As she matures, her self-confidence grows. She becomes a better judge of character and is not as likely to choose a man for the wrong reasons. She still gets her sense of importance from the opposite sex and her expectations of love are still a stumbling block. She needs so much love, recognition, and respect, she may spend half her life looking for the man who will give them to her—the one whose adoring love will last forever.

Her optimistic attitude and courage see her through many disillusionments and disappointments. Finally, she learns to examine her expectations and realizes she can give herself love and approval. When she no longer needs them from a man, she's ready for a healthy relationship.

She's a loving and generous person. She will take her elderly neighbor to the doctor in the morning, help out at the elementary school in the afternoon, and have energy left over to make a nice dinner for her family and oversee the children's homework.

She hates to lose contact with anyone, but she finally learns that people leave her life for sometimes unknown reasons, and she quits trying to dredge up old friendships.

At her best, she has become the kind of woman she always admired, the confident one who encourages and helps others succeed. She finds a way to express her vast creativity, not to impress, but for the satisfaction it brings. She has learned to truly love herself.

The Leo woman in love . . .

with an Aries:

A Leo woman and an Aries man can have more fun than two kids at Disneyland, and, in fact, that's one place they won't want to miss! They won't just paint the town red . . . they'll splash on every color in the rainbow. Once she's been with an Aries man, all other signs seem dull in comparison.

At first he's devoted and she basks in his love and attention, thinking, naively, it will always be like that. But when the dance is over, the Ferris wheel closes for the night, and the music fades, he's no longer totally focused on her. An Aries man gets tired of everything eventually, except perhaps Monday night football and having a good time with his pals.

A Leo woman doesn't take a back seat to anyone or anything, so she doesn't take this turn of events well. Obviously, he doesn't get it and she's not hesitant to let him know what she expects. Thus begins the battle of the wills with these two take-charge, don't-bring-me-down types. He isn't willing to give in, but she's more determined than he is: after all, this is her LOVE and her LIFE at stake.

Eventually they work out a compromise—or not. If he insists on his freedom, she accepts it grudgingly. But as long as she knows he loves her deeply, and he shows it at least some of the time, she will make the necessary attitude adjustment for the sake of the relationship.

If her worst fears come to pass and he is unfaithful, he'll have a wildcat on his hands, and he should not expect a second chance.

with a Taurus:

Being on the horns of a dilemma might describe a Leo woman hopelessly in love with a stick-in-the-mud Bull. There's more than a touch of Hollywood to the way a Leo woman wants to experience love, but her romantic expectations won't last long when she really gets to know a Taurus man.

She wants romance, sweet talk, candlelight dinners, unexpected surprises, and all the little touches that fit with her sense of drama. The Taurus man knows diddly squat about drama. The only time he gets dramatic is when the morning newspaper doesn't hit the porch on time.

Also, he won't change his opinion or his habits, not even for her! Just getting him to clean up and go out to someplace nice takes persuasion, bribery, or negotiation.

But still, there's so much to like in this man: he's dependable and can be counted on to do what he promises, which is refreshing after some of the harrowing experiences she's had with men. He's not likely to do something unforgivable that turns their marriage into a train wreck. Plus, the older she gets, the more she realizes that life is never going to be perfect, and once she's found a faithful mate, she isn't going to throw him away without making a huge effort.

For his part, he will learn to do the little things that make her happy, because he's practical enough to know it's in his own best interests. Her warmth, generosity, and gentle tenderness are worth the world to him. They have their share of arguments, and they can both be stubborn, but if they are committed, they can work out the kinks.

with a Gemini:

A Leo woman needs to know she is number one with her man and that he values and loves her deeply. With a Gemini man, this won't be obvious, because his actions seem to contradict his words. For one thing, he always has lots of friends, both men *and* women. He thrives on his social contacts, and anyone is fair game to talk and interact with.

There will be some rocky times with this couple until she accepts he is the way he is and she can't change it. Just because she is never going to have all his attention, it doesn't mean he doesn't love her; he just lives at a fast pace and needs to keep moving. He talks fast, thinks fast, probably works two jobs, and has at least one main interest or hobby. Fascinating, yes, but predictable, never.

Once she accepts his rapid-fire personality, she can decide not to be offended or hurt when he tells her he had lunch with a woman friend and how interesting she was, or when she watches him work the room at a party.

Their differences won't bother him much at all, so it's she who adapts if anyone does. Of course, it goes without saying that he *must* be loyal, both physically and mentally. If he is, they can share their many mutual interests and have much common ground on which to build a life together.

with a Cancer:

A Leo woman is attracted to a Cancer man when he speaks highly of his mom. A guy who appreciates family has become a top priority of hers, since her heart has already endured major repairs.

She discovers he has stayed at one job for years and she likes that about him, although sometimes she wonders if he could make more money by changing companies. But she wants security too, and so they settle into an intimate relationship and move in together.

At first it's good. He doesn't come right out and say so, but she knows he appreciates her considerable efforts to make him happy. She would like him to tell her more often, but, nevertheless, she feels loved and needed by him. Plus, he shares the chores and child care without a fight.

Then she discovers he can be moody. She likes to be happy and upbeat, so she tries to fix the problem. Figuring out what's wrong with him when he doesn't want to talk about it gets old. So life with him isn't all she thought it would be, but at least she feels secure in his love. If she has a high-status job and she can help him succeed in his job, the satisfaction she reaps will add much to her happiness.

For his part, he will have to toughen up a little and get used to her authoritative behavior because humble, she's not. Their relationship will require sacrifices and adjustments on both sides, but that's what marriage is all about.

with another Leo:

"I love you the most."

"No, I love *you* the most!"

Ah, the sound of two Leos who have discovered the secret to a happy union. These love bugs are quite content, snuggled up together, telling each other how wonderful they are.

They both need praise and a "thanks a lot!" for their good deeds. If he is mature, he realizes she has the same need for appreciation and recognition that he does. She, of course, will have to give the most. The Leo woman can dominate all other signs except the Leo man. Testosterone ramps up his need for recognition and applause, so she finds herself in the cheering section most often.

If he is arrogant or demanding, it takes all her nobility and strength to want to keep going. No Leo woman wants to feel she is in an inferior position. She learns to leave him alone at such times, which is punishment for him, because without an audience, he's lost.

Something that could undermine their marriage is over-spending and the resultant credit card debt. They both love nice things and it's hard when neither uses restraint.

Her career is wonderful for her, but not so great for him, especially if she makes more money or has more prestige. But these two just plain feel good in each other's company. They share a sense of fun and an enjoyment of the good life. Let's hear it for them! (The crowd roars its approval!)

with a Virgo:

They will both need to do their part if this twosome is going to have a better chance than the proverbial snowball in hell! A Leo woman has a good amount of pride in herself and her appearance, so it comes as quite a shock to hear a Virgo man make less than adoring comments about her hair or her outfit or anything else.

If he throws cold water on her dreams and calls them impractical or "pie in the sky," there's trouble afoot: She's trying to believe in herself and she needs her partner to believe in her, too. But he's hardwired to analyze everything, and he doesn't let even a wisp of optimism cloud his measured judgment.

One other thing: she can't help but notice that the Virgo man is, well, as cheap as a Wal-Mart sweater on clearance. She can't stand stinginess or pettiness. She wants to look great and live well, so she has a hard time staying within the budget. This can cause arguments galore because he hates waste and deplores extravagance.

He's too fussy for her as he frets over small details that aren't even on her radar screen, and even though he puts on a good front, he doesn't have a sense of his real worth. She feels she has to be constantly building him up and protecting his ego, a tiresome deal for a Leo woman.

This relationship can possibly work *if* she learns to not take things personally (doubtful) and he learns to *never* put her down in front of others (iffy, at best).

with a Libra:

So the Libra man isn't always totally sincere—at least he knows the right thing to say to make a girl feel good. And so what if he pretends everything is hunky dory when it isn't? At least he doesn't criticize and complain like some signs. With a Leo woman, if the balance of power is tipped in her direction, all the better. A Libra man is likely to let her have her way, which she knows is not because she's bossy, but because she's right.

So what are the stumbling blocks with this pair? First, there's the attention his charming self gets from the opposite sex. A Leo woman wants to be the only star in his sky. Then there's his reaction to the attention *she* gets from other men: why isn't he jealous? Actually, he is, but he doesn't let on. He doesn't want to cause a scene.

On the plus side, these two share a love of beauty. He has an eye for decorating, and her tastes run to the expensive, yet elegant. They will spend a lot of money on their home and will host gatherings of friends and family for all occasions. Unfortunately, they may overspend and end up with ferocious credit card debt that can topple their ideal existence.

They'll have their arguments, as all couples do, but they can usually work them out, unless one of them is very unhappy in the marriage. If it's him, there will be someone waiting in the wings for him—he doesn't do well as a solo act.

with a Scorpio:

His sarcastic, take-no-prisoners style is attractive to a Leo woman, who is a sucker for a commanding personality. She likes the way he's so adamant about what he likes and what he doesn't. Why is it that sometimes the very traits that attract a woman are the same ones that turn her off later?

A Leo woman will have to accept a Scorpio man as is because he isn't going to change to please her—not one iota. That strong will she admired can, and will, be used against her at some point.

She is warm and generous with him and expects the same treatment. She isn't prepared when he forgets her birthday. She needs praise and recognition, but he doesn't make much of even her incredible accomplishments. He isn't forthcoming with the sweet, encouraging words women love to hear. He's the guy who says, "You know I love you—so I don't have to say it." In the case of a Leo woman, he couldn't be more wrong.

Anger, tears, pressure—she tries them all but he doesn't budge. He hates scenes, and will leave if he gets too uncomfortable, not even giving her the satisfaction of venting her feelings in a resounding argument. If a battle is really serious, he'll ignore her tears and return her threats with icy silence.

The thing that can keep these two together is their mutual loyalty. Neither wants to bounce around and try out this person or that. They need someone they can trust and, hopefully, the Scorpio man is as physically loyal as he is mentally loyal. She may never know everything that's going on inside his heart, but as long as they both feel that bond between them, they're staying together.

with a Sagittarius:

In a Sagittarius man, a Leo woman has finally met her, dare we say . . . soul mate? That may be overstating it, but he *does* put a light in her eyes. He is generous and warm like her, and they are attracted to each other's love of life. Together they feel like they can be themselves. Of course, everyone else's love seems perfect and fabulous from a distance, and even these two will have their challenges.

Just as she wants flowers occasionally, he wants to have time with his buddies without having to justify being away for a few hours. That's just one concession she has to make with this outrageous but lovable guy.

He doesn't have a bit of stinginess about him. He does everything in a big way . . . eats, plays, spends, and jokes. He gives money to his friends or anyone else who needs it. If she tries to put limits on him, he'll find a way around them.

He's got a tendency to open his mouth before he thinks, and sometimes he blurts out the too-honest truth. She gets her feelings hurt, especially around other people. He thinks he was just being funny or teasing, but it isn't funny to her.

If he's one of those Archers who can be loyal, they will be the couple people point to while trying to convince themselves that true love is possible. If he's not, this is one lady who isn't going to overlook his philandering. Then he'll have another big thing in his life—a big alimony payment!

with a Capricorn:

A Leo woman wants a fun-loving guy, someone who makes her laugh and puts some excitement in her life . . . when she's young. After she's had some experience with love, she begins to look beyond the good times and ponder what's really important. Children will be near the top of the list, unless she's filled that space with nieces, nephews, or the children of her best friend. At this point in her life, the Leo woman could do worse than the unexciting, but stable and apt to be well-off, Capricorn man.

Both of them are strong personalities, but hers is basically sunny, while he suffers chronic self-doubt. He's a hard worker who strives to improve his position and attain financial security. He admires the way she manages her career and takes care of the children.

She is much warmer and more generous than he is. She plans extravagant parties and loves to entertain. He thinks entertaining, like golf, is just another way to make good business contacts. Still, they do like the same things, if for different reasons.

In time she learns that if she wants to go someplace that he doesn't want to go, she can pick up the phone and make arrangements with a friend. He might not give her everything she requires, but she is smart enough to realize when she's got it good. As long as she knows he deeply loves and respects her, she can make do with his less-than-entertaining style.

with an Aquarius:

An Aquarius man is part hunk, part oddball. He's different and she can't quite figure him out, so a Leo woman is instantly attracted to him. He seems like her type: someone who is interesting and likes to get out and have some fun.

They both enjoy people and social events, although for different reasons. She loves to buy a new outfit and show up looking wonderful and knowing she does. She enjoys seeing friends and keeping up on personal relationships.

He's a funny guy who makes any gathering into a party and loves to talk and laugh with friends. He loves a debate or discussion. He has a great memory for trivia and an endless curiosity about life. There are few things he hasn't studied, read about, experienced, or at least thought about. But he isn't tuned into people's feelings. His humor often has a bite to it and he doesn't mind getting a laugh at someone else's expense. A Leo woman is always aware of people's feelings and sometimes she flinches at the things that come out of his mouth.

It's easier for them to be friends than lovers. In fact, being friends comes easily to an Aquarius man; being half of a romantic couple just isn't him. Obviously, she needs a close bond more than he does. When they fight, it will often be about his wandering off to do his own thing.

If they work together for a joint purpose, and that can be a home and family or a business, it will take sincere effort and a bit of wisdom to make it work, but they can do it.

with a Pisces:

A Pisces man is so cuddly, she wants to give him a squeeze. When he takes her to a romantic little out-of-the-way place, she's hooked, sucker for love that she is, especially when she discovers what an attentive and sympathetic listener he is. Plus, he's comical and keeps her laughing, which she loves more than anything.

He doesn't need anyone's approval, so he won't compete with her to be the center of attention. She can be domineering at times, which threatens many men, but a Pisces man doesn't mind if she takes the limelight. In fact, he's attracted to her strength and is probably hoping she can give him some direction. She's as generous as can be and happy to help anyone, so they fit together quite nicely in that aspect. But although she's sympathetic, she can't sustain compassion forever. She wants a man she can be proud of, who is strong in his own right. If he leans on her too much, her sympathy gets exhausted, and she loses respect for him.

Another problem might arise if he is one of those injured Fish who is a dangerous game-player. A Leo woman can be badly hurt if she doesn't realize she is participating in the self-created drama of his life. He is so complex it's hard to know what his real motivation is, and it can take a long time to find out he isn't who he says he is.

THE VIRGO WOMAN
AUGUST 23–SEPTEMBER 22

The beautiful thing about a Virgo woman is that she's always changing and evolving. It's her nature to move toward perfection, and even though she knows it isn't really possible, that doesn't deter her from striving toward it.

As a young woman, she's a worrier. She worries about her pimples, her height, her looks, and her weight. If she develops early, she worries because she doesn't look like the other girls. If she's a late bloomer, she worries that she'll never get boobs. When she gets older, it's more of the same. She worries that she'll never find love, or that if she does, it won't last.

As she matures, she becomes more comfortable in her own skin, more confident in her abilities. She begins to accept herself, but it's a process that's never completed, because she can't help but see every flaw. She doesn't realize how competent she is and how well she does every task she takes on.

As she continues to grow in years and experience, she analyzes the way she handled situations, and the next time improves on it. She played by the rules; for example, she never took the labels off pillows that said, "Do not remove under penalty of law." She didn't think it was meant for her, but she didn't want to take any chances. It was for Virgo-types they added "except by the consumer."

When it comes to love, she learns to take her time and be more selective. She learns what type of man she can be happy with, and which ones she should turn down. She gains in self-confidence, but she still underestimates her attractiveness.

She can't remember a time when she hasn't worked, out of necessity, yes, but she admits her job is very important to her. Sweet, unassuming, and reserved, who would suspect the extent of her capabilities? Surely not she! In time, she learns to give herself credit for her industry and talent, and that's when she really comes into her own.

Being a Virgo woman isn't easy, but it gets easier as time goes on. She gets better at taking care of herself, and avoiding situations that aren't right for her. She doesn't offer her services so freely anymore to everyone who asks.

With men, she's attracted first by a meeting of the minds. The emotional attachment comes later, if she feels safe and isn't turned off. When she finds the right one, she is a devoted and faithful partner, willing to do anything in service to her loved one. That doesn't stop her from wanting to improve him, however. Learning to accept things and people the way they are is her greatest challenge, and yet, it is the most valuable thing she can achieve.

The Virgo woman in love . . .

with an Aries:

If a woman wore a white, long-sleeved, button-down blouse with a cherry red leather micro-mini, it would be like pairing a Virgo woman with an Aries man—they just don't go together. Oh sure, the Aries man is exciting. He makes a Virgo girl feel beautiful, and brings her out of her shell. She doesn't need the limelight, but is fascinated by someone who does. But once the passion has ebbed, she wonders what they have in common, other than the obvious.

If he shows his temper, she's tense. If he drives too fast, she's on edge. If they're with a boisterous crowd, she's uncomfortable. The whole experience starts to wear on her nervous system.

If they're on a road trip, she worries if they have enough gas, or wonders if the tires are sound or if he brought a map. He's not the type to prepare for an emergency, or even consider one. He does everything at full throttle, and he laughs at her silly concerns.

She worries if he doesn't wear his motorcycle helmet or if he's hiking without a first-aid kit. He never seems to be frightened or insecure—and that frightens her and makes her feel insecure. What she really needs is someone quiet and steady, a hard worker, like her, who is a little more predictable. So one day, she looks in the mirror and asks herself, "What was I thinking?"

with a Taurus:

A Virgo woman doesn't put up with any hanky panky and a Taurus man is more likely than most to be faithful. He usually won't risk his security by playing around. These are two practical people whose general views of the world are in agreement. Their values are working hard, keeping promises, taking care of business, paying the bills on time, putting something away for the future . . . nothing too exciting, just the elements of a structured and orderly life.

She won't demand the attention some women need, or think less of him for wanting to stay home a lot. He shows her how much he loves her by working hard. Bringing her flowers seldom occurs to him, and she doesn't expect it.

Once in a while, she does like an intellectual discussion. Unless the subject concerns him directly, he isn't a good candidate. For that, she may have to turn to her more verbal friends.

A big turnoff for her is if he wears unsightly old clothes around the house and doesn't shave on the weekends. She soon sets him straight on that! A big turnoff for him is if she works too many hours. He wants to eat at a certain time and isn't happy if it's a TV dinner. But she, ever the efficient one, probably has something homemade in the freezer just for occasions like that.

They can have a happy life together. He appreciates her green thumb and they both enjoy a garden, even if it's just growing tomatoes on the patio.

with a Gemini:

He's a kid at heart who obviously needs discipline, as only a Virgo woman can provide. Honesty and integrity are her hot buttons. While he's not exactly dishonest, he adapts to any role people want him to play and he's so glib and hard to pin down, who knows what the actual truth is?

Things that bug her: people who do crazy things that don't make any sense and people who are always late or don't show at all. That's him.

Things that bug him: anal people who are uptight and keep their house spotless. That's her. See the trend here? Everyday life is challenging, even though they do have plenty in common.

For one, they are both very smart. They love to read, although hers is self-help or good literature and his is the sports page or reading up on one of his many interests. They both enjoy traveling, but she likes to plan carefully and make reservations, while he wants to take off and decide where they'll stay once they arrive. They are both good with their hands and can enjoy art, crafts, and hobbies, although she tries to make it perfect and is dissatisfied with the results, while he tosses it off and calls it good.

They both change jobs fairly often, but she always has a good reason for quitting while he just likes a change.

If they go their separate ways, she may have a broken heart, but at least she's happy to be rid of all his stuff that was cluttering up the place. Some things feel as good as an orgasm!

with a Cancer:

Cancer is one of the best signs for a Virgo woman. They both love children, and they want at least one animal to care for and love, although she'll do most of the caring for. The only thing she insists on is that they don't smell (the pets *and* the kids).

He's another guy who likes to lounge around the house in his grody old clothes. If she tells him sweetly, so it doesn't hurt his feelings, to get cleaned up, he might. If he refuses—well, she won't be happy.

They both love their home and appreciate peace and quiet. She is happy with someone to pamper and wait on, and he just laps it up. She keeps an orderly house, even though she works and they take turns cooking.

They can do nicely running a business together because they com-plement each other's talents. He's a good people-person and planner, and she does the books and bills and handles the details. They are both good money-managers.

She knows a lot about nutrition and health and will nag him about his diet or how much he drinks. He is private and somewhat secretive and keeps things to himself. If she can let him go off and be alone without thinking it's because he doesn't love her, he'll love her all the more. Maybe he'll even put on a shirt.

with a Leo:

A Leo man can be the sunshine in the life of a Virgo woman. He just plain makes her feel good. She puts duty first, and often doesn't take time to enjoy life. He can show her how it's done. He sings a cheerful song and, before she knows it, she's humming along. He knows how to make her feel loved and appreciated, just what she desperately needs!

She expresses her love by doing things for her mate, so she gladly waits on him, cleans the house, cooks the meals, and even runs his bath. If she becomes almost a servant to him, at least she has a gener-ous boss. She's content in a supporting role as long as she feels loved. He needs recognition and it's second-nature to her to protect his ego.

And the downside? If she isn't appreciative or doesn't praise him enough, the Lion will not be content. She has a tendency to find fault and her criticism, though well-intentioned, will injure him more than she can know. She would be wise to bite her tongue and save her criti-cal comments for the important issues. For his part, he will spend money on expensive items that she doesn't think they need or can af-ford. But then he'll praise her when she feels she's done nothing and she's actually done a lot, and she needs someone to point that out to her. Or she makes something with her own two hands, something very special, just for him. And they decide to keep going.

with another Virgo:

These are two workaholics without a 12-step meeting—no time. The question is, with their busy schedules, will they ever see each other? Maybe, but their Saturday-night date is probably at the gym. Since they're more cerebral than physical, they keep quitting their exercise programs and then re-starting them out of guilt. Even so, they understand what they need to do to stay healthy.

They're both brainy and intellectual and enjoy reading, puzzles, and word games.

There's one thing they always agree on, and that is how important their work is: they both judge themselves by how they perform on the job. When one of them has to work late, or travel, or have the boss for dinner, the other understands.

They're both particular about what they eat, but that's not to say they have the same taste in food, just that each has his or her own definite opinions. They may even eat totally different meals.

They keep a fastidious home and neither is comfortable with less. Both are fanatical about something—for instance, his clothes are hung in like groups with the hangers spaced exactly two inches apart, and she keeps the towels stacked and sorted by color—compulsive things like that. But they *get* each other.

Neither is particularly easy to live with. They're always looking for ways they can improve . . . their partner! What neither needs is someone to point out *their* flaws. Nevertheless, here are two people who know what is meant by having to *work* at your marriage, so even when the going gets tough, these two won't quit. They just roll up their sleeves and get back to work.

with a Libra:

When a Libra man walks in, dressed to impress and smelling oh-so-good, a Virgo woman almost wants to jump his bones. When he speaks, she's even more interested because he's obviously intelligent and thoughtful.

They hit it off right away—her with her sweet smile and pleasant demeanor, and he with his charm and thoughtfulness. He takes her out to social events she would never attend by herself. On his arm, she feels more attractive and more confident. His friends, and he has many, are now her friends, and she enjoys parties like never before. Usually content to be in the background, she now looks at life, and herself, a little differently.

They both care about appearances and what people think of them. She can adapt to whatever he wants, anything from the girl next door to a sophisticated lady. He's witty and always knows the right thing to say.

People say she's hard to please, but not for a Libra man; he seems to have the knack. Their intimacy may be more tender than passionate, and that may suit them both. And they'll never offend by being coarse or unrefined.

He won't criticize her, thank God, because she does enough of that herself. But if she ever finds out he hasn't been totally honest with her, she'll be beyond hurt. Both have difficulty expressing anger, but if he's unfaithful, she'll find a way!

with a Scorpio:

Leave it to a Virgo woman to solve the enigma of the Scorpio man! If anyone can do it, she can. Actually, no one can, but she comes closer than most.

What about their love life? Isn't he the sex machine and she, the Virgin? It isn't as puzzling as it seems. A Scorpio man isn't more addicted to sex than any other sign; he just takes it more seriously. Having sex is letting someone know personal things about him that could be used against him later.

And a Virgo woman is not the eternal virgin; she's an earthy creature who is as highly sexed as most signs, more than many. These are, however, two people who don't exactly go out of their heads during sex. He is controlled about it, and part of her will remain untouched, so there is a certain holding back. Still, they can have a satisfying sex life.

She can be hurt by his coldness, because she needs more encouragement and love than he may give her. He's capable of loyalty, however, so she has to remember that faithfulness is more important than a kiss or a pat or a gift on Valentine's Day.

She's capable of making comments that cut him to the quick and that he will never forget. But when she is in love, she is devoted and will do anything for her mate. They just have to look beyond each other's faults and they will find what they have both been looking for . . . a loving and loyal partner.

with a Sagittarius:

A Virgo woman is sick and tired when she falls for a Sagittarius man. She's sick of being conscientious and tired of being so serious all the time.

Regardless of how willing she is to let the good times roll, she never gets to his level of spontaneity. She accompanies him to a hot tub party, a Mexican village, a film festival, a Grateful Dead concert, a nude beach—well, maybe not a nude beach, but she has many memorable adventures with him. When it comes down to the nitty gritty, however, these two are miles apart in personality, style, and basic needs.

He wants her to travel on a moment's notice, but she needs weeks to get her schedule arranged. She's a finicky planner/worrier, while he's ready to plunge ahead on a gamble. She enjoys taking tours, guidebook in hand; he hates the confinement of a tour and the timetable involved. He likes to go mountain climbing or white-water rafting, but she would much rather read about it than go on the actual trip.

She looks for assurances in love, but alas, with a Sagittarius man, those sweet little words of love just aren't forthcoming. In fact, he seems to have an uncanny ability to say the wrong thing. Before long, they're hurling adjectives at each other like "irresponsible" and "hard to please."

She just isn't cut out for this "I need my freedom" guy, and if he consistently hurts or disappoints her, she may begin to realize he's not worth the strain on her nervous system. Even if she's in love with him, she still has to be able to live with him.

with a Capricorn:

A Virgo/Capricorn couple has a standing weekly date . . . to compare appointments and update their Day-Timers! It may not be the kind of life everyone wants, but it works for them. At least neither is likely to pout because the other one spends too much time at work. There are many ways these two are similar:

A Virgo woman loves to receive useful gifts, say a laptop or a Palm Pilot, even a book or a vacuum cleaner. A Capricorn man is the most likely to spend his money wisely on just such things.

She wants to plan for the future—he has had a plan for his life since kindergarten. She has a need to be useful and can't imagine not working. He wants to get ahead and save for the future. She questions herself when shopping and analyzes every purchase. Is it practical? Is it quality? Will it last? The very questions he would ask.

They may not reach any blissful heights of passion, but then again, who says they won't? They are both down-to-earth and have an innate animal instinct, even though they appear very conservative to the casual observer.

The Virgo woman can administer a household, manage the budget, and raise the children so expertly that even the picky Capricorn man has to be impressed.

The danger here is a lopsided life, too much work and not enough fun. But when the mortgage is paid off and they still have years to enjoy their retirement, they get the last laugh.

with an Aquarius:
A Virgo woman believes in following the rules, while an Aquarius man never met a rule he didn't want to break. She's punctual and orderly while he's either late or doesn't get there at all.

Some of his schemes strike her as unrealistic, and she's just the one to see the devil in the details. She is usually humble and unassertive, so he's taken aback when she delivers one of her pointed comments about the flaw in his thinking or the glitch in his plans.

She is always ready to volunteer her services to a cause she believes in, and oftentimes, so is he. If they can just agree on who to help and how, they can use their humanitarian instincts as a common bond on which to build a satisfying life.

He joins groups to meet with like-minded people and discuss whatever the subject at hand requires. She doesn't mind attending meetings when they have a goal and a purpose, so she gets involved with his groups and committees. She isn't as thrilled when it's a purely social occasion, but with him, she has someone to break the ice and help her feel comfortable.

They are both good debaters and defend their ideas, but she may take it personally and feel attacked, while he is detached and enjoys stimulating disagreements. When things go wrong, she blames herself and he brushes it off and goes on with his life. This is a romance that wasn't made in heaven, unless it was so they can each learn tolerance.

with a Pisces:

A Virgo woman wants to be of service and a Pisces man is happy to let her. She's sweetly willing to do whatever she can to help him so she hunts down a CD he's been looking for, takes care of his dog when he's out of town, and straightens up his apartment.

She finds herself subconsciously attracted to men looking for a strong woman to lean on.

Okay, so all Pisces men aren't needy; but they do live in their own world and most regular folks have trouble following their thought processes. They can either be way up, or way down. He can be an intuitive CEO, or a hopeless drug addict. Either way, the depths of his inner life don't translate well into everyday responsibilities.

Can this practical girl be happy with a dreamer, and a disorganized one at that? She can decipher a complicated personality quicker than most, but with him—well, she has a better chance of understanding the theory of relativity.

They get along well and feel comfortable with each other, so in some ways, say in bed, they're good together. But in other ways, trouble lurks. If he lends money too freely to every friend in need, she nags him about his own responsibilities. When she nags him, he escapes to a more peaceful place. If there he finds an understanding woman who shows sympathy for his situation, that's bad. If he returns to talk about their disagreements and work them out, that's good—and it may be a new beginning. There is often a strong bond between these two that keeps them together, even through the hard times.

THE LIBRA WOMAN
SEPTEMBER 23–OCTOBER 22

The Libra woman was the cute little girl whose kindergarten teacher noted she plays well with others. She was popular and could persuade the other kids, nicely, yet convincingly, to do her bidding. She held court as the little princess, and always looked forward to marrying her prince.

As young as three, she loved putting on a fancy dress and shiny shoes for a party. She surprised her mom later by remembering everyone there, including the adults and who they were with. Her precocious interest in people and her affinity for beautiful things would stay with her throughout her life.

The teenaged Libra is a good student, often plays an instrument and loves to read, but her studies can't compare to her interest in people, boys in particular, and her preoccupation with makeup, hairstyles, and clothes. She knows how to make the most of her natural beauty. She's friendly and good-natured and lets her friends decide what movie to see or where to eat. She rarely lets people know if she's depressed or lacks confidence.

As she matures, the obsession she had with clothes as a teenager segues into a real talent for seeing the beautiful and harmonious in decorating, jewelry, art, accessories—anything with which she can express her style and sophistication. At some point, she will help others add beauty and elegance to their lives, either in a career or as a pastime.

The Libra woman's dilemma is that while she is ultra feminine, she thinks like a man and knows what she wants. As she matures, she hones her diplomatic skills and learns well how to handle people—think of her as part Southern belle and part cutthroat lawyer. First she dazzles with her beauty, then impresses with her quick mind, and, finally, seals the deal with the right words.

She knows how to play the game, and that includes the game of love. But getting a man isn't the problem. Being satisfied with what she has often is. She wants nothing less than the best life has to offer—a lovely home, beautiful furnishings, money, plus a loving, generous partner who impresses her friends and family, who knows what she needs to be happy and gives it to her. Most young men, and many older ones, can't offer all that.

In her search for Mr. Right, she dates married men, has monogamous affairs and even has relationships with several men at the same time. She tries out different lifestyles and tilts from one extreme to the other trying to find the balance in herself and her life.

She gives wise counsel to her friends, but has a hard time taking her own advice. In spite of her beauty, she comes up short in her own eyes because she's so aware of how people perceive her. There's always something to improve, or someone new to impress.

In her wisdom as a mature woman, she knows enough about herself to realize she put too much energy into being what other people want her to be. She knows she can't find self-esteem in a relationship. Once she quits waiting for a man to give her everything, she's entered a new phase. She begins to cultivate her mind and find success in a career that's right for her. She has polished her outside image and developed peace and harmony within. She has grown into an awareness of her deep desire for intimacy and is able to commit to one less-than-princely soul. And that is when she can fulfill her destiny and merge into a true partnership as a giving, loving woman. If it's not to be, she's a survivor who has recognized her strength, and knows she can take care of herself.

The Libra woman in love . . .

with an Aries:

Opposites always attract, but never more than when a Libra woman, the most feminine sign, meets an Aries man, the most masculine. Before she can say, "Should I or shouldn't I?" she's in love.

With him, she doesn't have to worry about being pressed to make a decision; he'll make them all. But he'd best not confuse her good nature with being a pushover. Her iron hand is in a velvet glove and he won't even know he's being handled as she gently persuades him to see things her way.

He could use some of her tact. She's appalled at the way he doesn't seem to notice or care about the effect he has on people with his arrogance, including her. She needs to be treated gently, but he isn't exactly Mr. Sensitive, and he can hurt her without realizing it.

As for him, he'll be puzzled and surprised when he discovers she's holding a grudge over something he thought was over and done with. He's forgotten about it, why can't she?

He'll finish her sentences, talk about himself all night, and won't give her time to make a well-thought-out decision. For her part, she'll test his patience when she takes forever to decide what to order at a restaurant, and when she doesn't tell him what she really thinks, until it's too late. Not unexpected result: it can work, but she'll have to have a lot of tolerance.

with a Taurus:

She loves to go out, be seen, and schmooze with the beautiful people. He's more the beer bar or billiards palace type who enjoys a casual get-together in comfortable clothes. At first, he attends parties and goes places with her, but as the relationship progresses, he starts to make excuses because he would really rather stay in and watch sports with a bucket of chicken. This won't be an easy dilemma to solve because she isn't going to play earth mother for anyone, no matter how big a hunk he is.

His quiet moods can frustrate her, because stimulating conversation is one of her greatest enjoyments. He doesn't understand much of what goes on in her complicated mind because his needs are more simple: a secure income, good food, a peaceful domestic life, good sex. He doesn't have a clue how much spunk, energy, and purpose are behind that sweet exterior of hers.

Still, when they're at home, just the two of them, they share a love of comfort and beauty. When she sets the mood with soft music, sweet-smelling perfumes, bath oils and powders, and satin sheets on the bed, he's willing to do almost anything, and he'll have to if he wants to keep her happy!

with a Gemini:

For a Libra woman, a Gemini man is like a tornado blowing into town: she never knows where he'll touch down next. He's unsettling and intriguing at the same time.

They love to compare ideas and discuss everything from the price of gas to where they like to eat. They can stay up all night listening and talking. So she listens more and he talks more, what's new?

He has a hunch he's met the perfect woman, smart enough to be interesting and sweet enough to love. At some later date, he will realize that her softly feminine demeanor overlays a strong will, and that no matter how sweetly she does it, she always seems to get her own way. But it will be well after the wedding silver begins to tarnish before he figures it out.

Their biggest problem occurs when she loses trust in him, one of the pitfalls with a Gemini man. It's not that he isn't truthful, but when she sees how easily he can manipulate any situation to his advantage, she begins to have her doubts about his sincerity. Trying to keep up with where he is and what's next on his agenda is way too much work for her, and hard on her nervous system as well; she didn't think it would be this difficult.

Still, they can be great friends, and if anyone can come up with a plan they can both agree to, they can—but it may take all her diplomatic skills.

with a Cancer:

These two signs both like to take the lead, but neither likes to show it, which can lead to all manner of misunderstandings and injured feelings. If only they could come out with it already! The Cancer man bottles up his feelings, so no one knows what's upset him. The Libra woman doesn't want to make waves by bringing up unpleasant subjects, so no one knows she's upset. All this controlled upsetness can put their marriage on life support. Gee, wonder why?

Sometimes a good lively argument is what's needed to clear the air. Unfortunately, that's not in either of their stylebooks. More likely is a short and nasty blow-up followed by icy silence. Where's Dr. Phil?

She loves to dress up and go places, but he's a homebody. If she can just get him to put on the new clothes she bought for him, she can surely convince him to go to the ball with her womanly charms. Maybe if she bakes a cherry pie? Actually, that might work!

Nevertheless, they do have times when they meet in the middle. She'll have their home amazingly decorated in harmonic colors and subtle patterns. Even on a budget she can work wonders, and he'll love it.

Their two biggest difficulties: (1) She loves to buy beautiful things, and he is, shall we say, thrifty? (2) He needs tender encouragement, and she isn't always in the mood to accommodate him.

with a Leo:

She thinks nothing is too good for her and he agrees! What a team. They enjoy similar lifestyles and share a fondness for luxury and good living. In best cases, they will acquire beautiful possessions, expensive clothes, and a home they will proudly show off to their friends.

She'll smother him with attention and adoration, and he, in turn, will give her expensive gifts and little surprises "just because I love you." Finances will be an issue if they accumulate too much credit card debt or otherwise spend beyond their means.

He loves her for her intelligence and attractiveness and proudly shows her off when they go out. He gets annoyed at a party if he thinks she's getting too much attention from other men, and it won't be in silence, either. But she gently reassures him that she's just being sociable and, assuming she's being truthful, he gets over it.

She encourages him when he doubts himself, and yes, Leo men *do* doubt themselves in spite of their egos. She doesn't mind doing things for him or being the one who usually gives in, because he shows her how much he loves her in so many ways.

This is one of the best signs for a Libra woman, and it's a lucky thing, because she was far too blissful in the first glow of romance to balance the good with the bad and make an educated decision. For her, life's simpler that way.

with a Virgo:

"How can he be so mean if he loves me?" It isn't easy for a tender Libra woman to be criticized by her Virgo partner because she tries so hard to make everything nice. But he has his definite ideas of how things *should* be and a habit of pointing out flaws. She cannot take a lot of criticism, well-intended though it may be. She is sensitive to what people think of her, and can't just brush it off.

The Libra woman needs a true partner who will escort her to the many events, meetings, and parties she loves to attend. She doesn't want to go alone, but if she has to drag him out against his will, she's not going to be a happy camper, and neither is he.

They'll soon discover their minds work in different ways. Even though they respect each other's intelligence, her habit of vacillating "Yes, no, maybe so" on her way to a decision is a waste of valuable time to him. He comes to a logical decision and then acts on it, simple as that.

On the plus side, he admires her artistic and decorating skills, and she appreciates his ability to remodel the family room or build a storage unit. They both like an orderly environment and she isn't happy in less than beautiful surroundings.

Maybe if she learns to ignore his unkind comments, and he agrees to accompany her to X places a month, they can keep this not-so-easy relationship out of critical condition.

with another Libra:

It's downright amazing how much these two talented people can accomplish together. They can run a business, decorate their home, work on a committee, or throw a party, and do it with flair and pizzazz. They bring their intelligence and good taste to bear on any project they take on, which puts them in great demand as a couple.

The Libra woman appreciates a man who knows how to present an impressive appearance, one who is well-groomed and smells nice. Of course, she knows how to dress for any occasion and always looks fantastic. Together they could be the king and queen of the homecoming ball, albeit a touch older.

Deciding where to go after the ball is not as easy. Coming to a mutual decision can be a lengthy process, what with all the weighing of pros and cons. But these two clever folks can find a way to work out most things; maybe she'll choose the restaurant and he can select the wine.

They assist one another up their social and career ladders and never have to worry about a partner who doesn't understand the unwritten rules. They both enjoy conversation and love to have someone to discuss the evening news with or share an insight about a book.

These two are such diplomats, it's hard to imagine them fighting. Can they live life on a superficial basis without ever dealing with issues? Who knows? Nevertheless, that's their style. If and when they do part ways, it won't be because they grated against each other's personality. It will be because one of them found someone else.

with a Scorpio:

When a Libra woman turns on her seductive charms with a Scorpio man, he's as defenseless as a computer without a firewall! He keeps his guard up at first because it's his manner to be distrustful, especially with a beautiful woman. But she's so alluring and interesting, he doesn't stand a chance unless he leaves town and never looks back. Bet on him throwing caution to the wind and going for it. Later she will tell her friends that she didn't know what she was getting herself into.

She loves to talk about everything under the sun and they seem to be having a great conversation, but she realizes later he was asking all the questions and she was supplying all the answers . . . especially about her past life. She should tread very carefully here because what she says can be used against her later.

If she ever says something that offends him she'll never know, until he throws her words back at her during an argument—maybe a year later. He's a tough one to figure out, even for someone as good with people as she is.

If he loves her deeply, he'll share more of himself with her than he has with anyone else, but that doesn't mean she can ever know him completely. She must vow never to discuss his personal business, because he values his privacy above all.

There are times when a Libra woman juggles more than one relationship. If she does this with a Scorpio and he finds out, he won't hang around to see who wins, not to mention other, uglier, consequences.

with a Sagittarius:

Most Sagittarius men are party animals, but pizza, beer, and a football game are not a Libra lady's idea of a party. If it's going to be boisterous, which it certainly will be, she might do something with a friend and leave the house to him.

He enjoys socializing, so he'll take her to her fancy parties and enjoy meeting people. But he loves to travel and does so at any opportunity so he's often away, and she hates to go anywhere alone.

He's good for her because he encourages her to relax and be more spontaneous. For instance, he might ask her to fly to Mexico in a friend's private plane, but she needs time to deliberate before making an important decision . . . okay, any decision.

He's funny and she loves his sense of humor, even if he blurts out inappropriate comments. He does it good-naturedly so people usually aren't offended. She's much more diplomatic and more aware of people's feelings; together, they make an interesting couple.

He's not just a gregarious guy who loves adventure. He's a thoughtful, philosophical seeker after knowledge as well. He has opinions and beliefs on many subjects. Even some of his friends don't know that about him, but she does.

With a few compromises and a little tolerance, a Libra woman and a Sagittarius man will get along fine. Hopefully, by the time they meet, he has already explored his more adventurous dreams. Whether or not to marry will be one of their more difficult decisions. Even he will have to think about that one.

with a Capricorn:

Ah, poetic justice . . . a Libra woman who loves the finer things in life on the arm of a Capricorn man, nicknamed in astrology, "the Diamond Buyer."

It's a Hollywood cliché: a wealthy man with a beautifully coiffured, dressed-to-the-nines, much younger woman who knows how to schmooze her way in any company.

That's great, but what if they are just ordinary people living an ordinary life? They all face the same challenges.

A Libra woman often chooses a man who is different from her. He could be of a different ethnic heritage, different social group, a lot older or younger. Even if they come from similar roots, however, they still have different personalities.

A Capricorn man is driven to succeed and can be a solitary overworker. She is much more of a people-person and needs to socialize more than he does. But if he thinks he can make some valuable contacts, he goes to social functions quite willingly. She loves to entertain, so she's an asset to him in that way.

He's careful with money and expects her to live within their budget, but she can go over her credit card limit before you can say, "SAVE 50 percent!"

He's old fashioned and some call him chauvinistic. Her approach to that is simple: she lets him believe he's getting his way. Manipulating (or influencing) people is one of her great talents. It beats confrontation and accomplishes the same thing.

with an Aquarius:

If you hear them in a lively debate, not to worry, they're enjoying it. He likes to be challenged with a different perspective—with a Libra woman, he will be. She has opinions and is eager to share, but neither gets all emotional about it.

She's good with people and is very considerate. She wants a companion because she isn't happy going places alone. He is more independent. He loves to have a lot of friends, but is more detached and less personally involved with them.

Both are informed about social or political issues. Even though they both value fairness and equality, they won't necessarily be on the same side, all the more opportunity for the pointed discussions they both enjoy. In fact, if they don't have enough intellectual stimulation, they get fidgety and restless. A tendency to argue might hide the deep devotion these two have for each other.

They could easily be over-booked. He is often busy with meetings or one of his unusual schemes, which might conflict with an event she doesn't want to miss. In that case, he won't mind if she is escorted by one of their gay male friends.

She will love to join him to promote his causes. Her ideal joint mission: a beautification project. It's what she excels at, and together they could make a real difference in their community.

No woman can make a man happier or be a better partner than a Libra woman who has found her mate, and an Aquarius man might just be the one. But if, for some reason, they split, they will always remain friends—count on it!

with a Pisces:

Compared to him, a Libra woman is decisive! She uses logic to put the pieces together. If it takes a while to come to a decision that is pleasing to all, at least she understands the issues.

A Pisces man is complicated and views life through the filter of his emotions. There's always another angle to consider so his opinions are hard to pin down, even for him.

Nevertheless, he's appealing to a Libra woman because he's agreeable and easy-going. She can't resist falling in love when he invites her to a play or concert and afterward takes her to a romantic little restaurant. He's fun to talk to and she basks in his undivided attention.

Of course, he falls for her in a big way—what man wouldn't? She's lovely to look at and they share an enjoyment of art, movies, and music; either or both may play an instrument.

She has an aversion to the seamier side of life, so she is somewhat shocked to meet some of his less desirable friends. He's a sucker for anyone in trouble and will give his last dollar to someone who needs it. She doesn't feel much sympathy for some of his hangers-on who, in her opinion, should pull themselves together and get a life.

He wants her to help him decide what path to take next. If he doesn't have many solid goals, she'll soon tire of playing nursemaid.

These two can have a long-lasting relationship, if for no other reason than neither wants to hurt the other's feelings. They may just drift apart, never making the final decision to break up.

THE SCORPIO WOMAN

OCTOBER 23–NOVEMBER 21

A Scorpio daughter was a challenge that only the parents of another Scorpio could understand. They discovered her strong will in her first few months. As she got older, she didn't realize she was just a kid; in her eyes she was anyone's equal and she resented rules and restrictions.

Even when her parents used firm discipline, they never felt they were making much of an impression on this headstrong little person. To reach her full potential later, she needed understanding even more than control. If she wasn't treated with love and respect, she could become shy and fearful, but she was fully capable, even as a child, to direct her own life and she had the will to do it.

She stood out from all the other little girls with their cute bows and sweet smiles. She had a magnetic quality about her that even adults noticed. She had a strong intuitive sense and a way of knowing things. She assumed everyone had similar experiences until she was older and realized she was, indeed, tuned into the mystical, unseen world.

If her parents promised her something and didn't follow through, or she thought they were unfair, she was deeply offended and carried the wound into adulthood.

As a young woman, someone may have controlled her in a negative way, but it never broke her spirit. In time, she did what she had to do to reclaim her life. She began to feel her own strength as she learned to rely on herself.

As she goes through life, she experiences many intense connections and several bitter breakups. Her relationships reflect her deepest needs and tend to go to extremes, first incredibly close and private, then open and casual. She has at least one major crisis that totally changes her. She deals with life and death issues, namely power, money, and sex, all of them connected to the most horrific acts—or the most sublime.

When she comes into her own, she explores the heights instead of the depths. She has forgiven others and herself. She knows what she wants, and what she doesn't. She may have conquered herself, or still be working on it, but the power she has to change her life is immense—so is her power to change others' lives for good or ill. She can recreate herself into a successful career woman, a devoted wife and mother, or a single woman pursuing her life's dream. She will do it with passion, dedication, and love, and will always lend her great strength when and where it is needed.

The Scorpio woman in love . . .

with an Aries:

If she wants a blistering hot romp in the hay, and of course she does, an Aries man is just her kinda guy. But fights are inevitable! A Scorpio woman isn't going to be tamed by a mere man, even a macho Aries. They're both domineering and want their own way, and yet they want someone who offers a challenge. Hmmm . . . sounds like a boxing match.

She'll play for a while, but eventually it will either come down to a noisy fight and breakup, or she'll tire of the game and split. No problem. When she's tempted by a lusty, sexy man, a Scorpio woman doesn't care if it's going to last forever!

An Aries man is an uncomplicated guy who takes life at face value. He wants to be himself, have fun, reach his goals, keep moving, and defeat all comers.

She's a complex person with strong feelings about everything. Her opinions, emotions, and desires are hard to decipher, even for her.

He has a quick temper that flares up quickly and is then forgotten. Her anger is controlled and icy and an injury is never forgotten.

She has a unique code of honor she lives by, and once she's given herself to someone emotionally, she expects full loyalty and faithfulness in return. An Aries man can have a hard time living up to her expectations. If he breaks her heart, she won't be around to let him do it again. And maybe he won't, either.

with a Taurus:

He's there to listen and calm her down when she's stressed. He offers her security in an unpredictable world. When everyone is against her, he's for her. A Scorpio woman can do much worse than a Taurus man. He may not take her to the heights of passion, but he's plenty sexy and physical in a straightforward way.

The Scorpio woman needs a strong, tolerant male who lets her be herself and doesn't judge her when she goes to extremes, as she is prone to do. He may not understand her strong opinions and volatile reactions, but he's patient and tolerant. It takes a lot more than a complicated wife to make him give up.

When she marries, the Scorpio woman wants it to be forever, and so does a Taurus man. Even though they are opposites in many ways, and will have many strong disagreements, they can stick it out through the hard times. He isn't willing to throw his security away without good reason, and she is totally loyal once she is committed.

Even if it's only finances or the children that keep them together at one point, they may someday discover that their relationship has become comfortable and satisfying after all. If she develops tolerance for his routines and doesn't expect him to fill all her needs, and he runs true-to-type and remains faithful, these two just might be stubborn enough to make it work.

with a Gemini:

A Scorpio woman may be the only one who can keep tabs on a Gemini man. Little does he know, but she put the "private" in private investigator. So just in case he was thinking of a questionable liaison with a "friend," he should know up front that he's not going to fool her for long.

She wants to be in control of her life. That's a valiant goal but a doomed one with a Gemini man, even if she doesn't suspect him of fooling around. He's always busy—so many places to go, so many people to see, so much to do. He has no end of plans and ideas he wants to try out, or may try out, or probably will just talk about. It's exhausting. And he's never the same. Sometimes he's talkative and pleasant, other times, cold and distant. One minute he's listening to her intently, and the next minute, he's flipping through the cable guide.

There isn't much common ground here. She lives by her instincts and emotions; he makes decisions based purely on logic. He likes to take the easy way, and she likes a challenge, which is probably why she picked him in the first place.

Once she has set herself a goal she won't give up, so it would be a mistake to rule this couple out entirely. If she has a career, children, and a few close friends to take up the slack, it might work, but only because when she sets her mind to something, anything is possible.

with a Cancer:

A Cancer man wants a safe and sane life, like New Year's Eve with no liquor. He wants his honey to be home, have his dinner ready, and always be the same sweet girl he married. Wrong! What she is today, the Scorpio woman may not be tomorrow. With her, there are no "for sures," except that she will live with intensity and gusto.

If she adopts the role of loyal helpmate and mother, she will still need an avenue through which to explore her sensuality—belly dancing, writing sexy stories, trying out new sexual aids—something that adds spice and passion to life. And she wants something deep and mysterious to ponder, like ghoulies and ghosties and long-leggedy beasties, or why the neighbors have so many late-night visitors.

Of these two private people, she's the most stubborn and he, en-
cumbered as he is with the male ego, the most sensitive. If, in one of
their rare fights, she stings him with her harsh words, he may withdraw
into his little crabby shell forever, proving that withdrawing, not fighting, is the most dangerous behavior in a relationship.

Humor can be a marriage-saver. One couple with these signs had a
wacky but workable solution to communicating hurt feelings and
touchy subjects. They used a little stuffed dog they named Iddy Boo to
remove themselves from their emotions. When one of them had something to get off their chest, he or she would pick up the dog, wag its
little head, and say, "Iddy Boo is sad because you were so rude last
night."

"Well, tell Iddy Boo I'm sorry—I was just tired." It worked for
them, and they are still married to this day.

with a Leo:

The kingly Lion will be ever-so-proud of his Scorpio mate, because
she can do it all! She is a giver who will organize her life to make him
happy, and see that he has everything he needs and wants, as much as
it's in her vast power to do.

She'll be a great hostess, indispensable business partner, wife, mom
and/or stepmom, and exotic lover. But she has to want to do it—or
she'll keep score and expect to be paid back.

He was immediately attracted by her competence and strength. She
was impressed by his generous nature and confidence—not to mention his great hair. They'll have some bumps in the road to maneuver
around, because both of them are mule-headed and determined. But
they know deep-down they can count on each other—and that is *the*
most important thing to either of them. He instinctively knows she
will be there when he needs her, and so does she—or she wouldn't be
willing to give 60 percent to make it work!

He basks in her love and attention, and she loves the way he makes
her feel special on birthdays and anniversaries. If he doesn't, he isn't
the brightest lion in the pride.

Neither is the type to give up easily, so they'll keep working on the flaws in their relationship. This is where their mutual stubbornness comes in—as long as they can count on one another to keep their word and they are both 100 percent loyal, everything else is negotiable.

with a Virgo:

The Virgo man has taken *smarts* to a whole new level; in fact, it's like his brain is a computer. When a Scorpio woman gets hold of him, she might just blow out his hard drive (no pun intended), meaning she can provide gigabytes of data with her intuition and instincts. If he takes advantage of her insights, he can become even more well-informed than he already is. But anything that isn't scientific fact is easy for him to dismiss.

He has an irritating way of setting out his arguments so accurately and precisely, it's impossible to argue. She knows how she feels, but can't explain it in crisp detail like he can. She's good at poker, though: she can match his logic and raise it one gut feeling and a hunch.

He wants to know everything and to organize it, name it, and define it. When he starts analyzing her and her deepest feelings and needs and advises her of his diagnosis, she'll have to sit him down and explain that it isn't nice to pry and, anyway, he doesn't know *everything*.

He's good with the kids and loves the dog, although he's a little too strict with the kids, won't walk the dog, and won't clean up after any of them. Ew, icky.

His tendency to notice every shortcoming and criticize those he loves can get him in big trouble, because she's hard enough on herself to begin with. If he's too critical too often, she'll leave, but not before she's given him plenty of warning.

with a Libra:

She is the exquisite hostess when they entertain their friends and business associates. She is the devoted and strong partner he so desires by his side. If he dislikes decisions, she is fully capable of making them. She is as diplomatic as he and she loves a stimulating discussion just as

much. So what are the potholes in the road for a Scorpio woman and
a Libra man?

1. She, who suffers from self-doubt in spite of her strong personality, needs a straight-talking guy because she can smell insincerity
   a block away. A Libra man tells people what they want to hear.
   A little of that is good, because who wants to know the complete,
   unvarnished truth? Depends on if the question is, "Does my butt
   look big in these pants?" or "Would you ever be unfaithful?"

2. He's a magnet for women because he's attractive, cleans up real
   nice, and knows how to charm the pants off . . . uh . . . charm
   the birds out of the trees. A Scorpio woman can see right
   through him, and is not going to be understanding if he's overly
   friendly. If he can't be the true-blue lover she needs, their union
   won't last.

If they stay honest with each other and don't hide their fears—well,
he's not always honest and she hides her fears—they could discuss how
they will handle a disagreement beforehand. Then if he goes in his office and shuts the door, she can remind him that they agreed to talk
and not withdraw.

with another Scorpio:

Two Scorpios who are meant to be together will recognize their intense attraction in the first few minutes of meeting. From that point,
they can go to the heights, to the depths, and back again, and probably
will.

Their best bet is to come together purely for sex. If they do, they
won't be disappointed. But if they fall in love and want to make it permanent, it gets a little trickier—a *lot* trickier, in fact.

Even though they have a powerful love affair, they have to deal
with their co-jealousy, and will watch each other like hawks, although
he will be the one most likely to go to extremes that only a crazed
male ego could invent. They will love intensely, fight intensely, and
take their relationship to the brink. Sex will be an issue in some way,
anything from promiscuity to impotency—too much or too little.

If one of them is betrayed, he or she will seek revenge, like the Scorpio woman who steered her car with one hand while scattering her lover's clothes all over Main Street with the other. Or the enraged ex who had cement poured into his girlfriend's convertible. Or even uglier stuff we don't want to think about.

They might consider these rules:

1. Never snoop around in each other's private stuff.

2. Never talk about ex-lovers or sexual exploits.

3. Vow to be totally honest and loyal—and do it!

It might take years, but it is possible to develop the trust each needs to feel safe. If they combine the best in themselves, their power can accomplish some great mission—even a long-lasting marriage.

with a Sagittarius:

Even when he's home and not off tramping through the mud on a duck hunt, she's got gripes. For one thing, she enjoys small groups of intimate friends, while he likes to get a crowd of friends and acquaintances together and party till dawn. A Scorpio woman isn't going to tolerate being ignored or taken for granted very damn long.

He has a generous heart and wants her to be happy—he truly does—but she'll soon figure out that his extravagant promises can't be counted on, and she'll resent it.

A Scorpio woman can become very emotionally attached to a Sagittarius man, and once she falls in love, she feels it with all the intensity of her loyal heart! A Sagittarius man likes to be unfettered, loose, free. He doesn't want to be weighed down by a strong attachment to anything except his dog; and even Yukon has to be fed every day (what a drag). Nope, settling down is not on his must-do list for this lifetime.

Since she's the one who will give the most, what can she do to be happy? For one, she can look to her job. She's ambitious and needs a demanding career, so the recognition and satisfaction she finds at work will help.

For a Scorpio woman who needs a strictly monogamous and loyal relationship, a Sagittarius man means settling for a different life than the one she was looking for, and it's not in her nature to settle.

with a Capricorn:

With a Capricorn man, a Scorpio woman is going to have to be forceful in a subtle way, which she is fully capable of doing. He's used to having authority and makes the mistake of thinking he can impose his opinion on her. Boy, does he have the wrong woman!

She is determined to pursue her goals as she sees fit and won't change to please him or anyone else. She's used to controlling people, not the other way around! Her only recourse to keep the peace is to use diplomacy and secret techniques (that only she knows) to handle him.

Overall, they respect each other's ambitions, but they may differ on method. He's as practical and down-to-earth as can be and doesn't believe in airy-fairy concepts that aren't proved. Naturally her mysterious ways are unfathomable to him. She has a lot to teach him, and if he's a smart Mountain Goat, he will be humble enough to listen and learn.

As far as faithfulness, he will think twice before putting his life (and bank account) in jeopardy for a little sex, especially when he's having good sex with her. He's as content as she is to spend a comfortable, cozy evening at home. He isn't romantic, and doesn't speak softly of his deep love or how he's enchanted with her—that's not his style. But she's intuitive and can sense when she is loved.

He admires immensely the way she doesn't give up, because he's the same way.

If they set their wills and their minds to accomplish something, only Fate could stand in their way; mere mortals could not.

with an Aquarius:

A Scorpio woman loves a mystery, and an Aquarius man isn't easy to typecast. When she first spied him, he was probably expounding at length on one of the many unconventional topics that catch his attention, anything from astrology, crop circles, Egypt, or chanting, to the healing workshop he just attended in California. Like her, he's drawn to mysteries and unexplained phenomena. He'll also have a cause he's passionate about, something he wants to change in the world, and so might she, because she's often an advocate for someone or some group that needs a spokesperson.

They are both opinionated and soon they are challenging each other with their ideas and beliefs. This will become a large part of their relationship. He admires her commitment and the way she dedicates herself to anything she believes in.

As time goes on, she discovers that, as much as he likes to talk, it's always on an impersonal level, never about him. She tends to be possessive and forms strong connections with people and needs a guy who can give back, but an Aquarian man likes his freedom, his friends, and his life as it is. He doesn't usually want a close relationship that involves commitment and entanglement—at least not until he's lived some.

If it just so happens he is ready to commit and settle down, he could become the loyal partner she needs. Otherwise, she should be satisfied to be lovers, because as much as they love to explore each other's inquiring mind, it doesn't translate into the kind of close personal bond she needs. Oh well, maybe they will meet again on the astral plane.

with a Pisces:

A Scorpio woman is the only one who can go to the depths of emotion and the heights of spirituality with a Pisces man. Most people don't discuss parallel universes and probable realities, but these two do. If he's into meditation or prayer, he can help her focus her immense psychic powers on the positive.

But that's if they are into such things, because not every Pisces and Scorpio is. Sometimes a Pisces man just goes through life bewildered because he can't progress in a straight line like most men. He seems to be the recipient of all the bad luck in the world and needs someone more organized to help him along.

He usually has some painful episode in his past from which he is recovering. A Scorpio woman is ready to lend her strength to anyone in need, and the worse off they are, the more determined she is to "fix" them. She doesn't mind if her mate is dependent on her; she's used to carrying the load.

Neither realizes, in the beginning, that this is the undercurrent that defines their relationship. Until this plays out, she feels she has found a kindred spirit, and she has. At heart, he's a poet, an artist, a seeker. He has dreams, fantasies, and secrets, just like her. Plus, he's sweet, lovable, and gives a great foot rub!

If he is emotionally healthy or nearly so, their chance of happiness will naturally increase. If he isn't loyal and honest, and she finds out, she'll drop the sweet little helpmate role in a hurry and he'll see a different side of her—the bitchy side—just before she grabs her tarot cards, slams the door behind her, and never looks back.

The Sagittarius Woman
November 22–December 21

You can hear her laugh before you see her, and the room brightens a little when she walks in. The Sagittarius woman has arrived—let the party begin! She always has an outrageously funny story to tell, and if it's on her, she laughs loudest of all.

As a young girl, she was well-liked at school, and if she wasn't beautiful enough to be the prom queen, she was popular and had lots of friends of both sexes. They liked her because she was friendly, funny, and audacious. She always had a big smile and could crack a joke or make a sarcastic comment with the best of them.

Her family moved a lot but she took it in stride, made new friends, and each time she learned a little more about new people and places. Perhaps because of that, she liked to read about exotic lands and imagine herself living there. She thought of bicycling through Europe instead of college for an education.

She got her first job as a teenager and loved the freedom a little money in her pocket gave her. She always spent it as soon as she got it, treating her friends to a movie or hamburgers and fries. She didn't save any, because she knew there'd be more where that came from, or from somewhere else.

She was never totally sold on being a wife and mother; it sounded limiting and boring. If she did happen to marry young, it was to get out of the house and it didn't last long.

Regardless of whether or not she graduated from college, her education never ends. Her bookshelves reflect the scope of her interests, and she takes classes about her current fascination.

She's had countless extraordinary experiences, both good and bad, and, whether or not she realizes it, she has always had a guardian angel. When her back is up against the wall, something always turns up, a family friend to give her a job, a source of tuition money, a mentor at work, or some lucky coincidence.

She's had many boyfriends, many affairs, and probably more than one marriage, but she always looks to the future, stays optimistic, and makes jokes about her past troubles, so even the poignant moments seem almost funny. Like Scarlett O'Hara, she believes tomorrow is another, brighter day.

Since she's matured, she's learned to take responsibility for herself and her dependents, be they children or animals. She has traveled as often as circumstances have allowed, and she still daydreams about far-away places she hasn't yet seen. But now the motive isn't to get away, but to expand her understanding of the world. Her love of adventure is still as strong as ever, but she has learned to tone down her exuberance with the wisdom born of experience.

The Sagittarius woman in love . . .

with an Aries:

An Aries man comes along just when the Sagittarius woman needs him, like a serendipitous gift. He banishes whatever concerns were bringing down her usually high spirits and puts a smile back on her face. The adventures they have will make for many great stories when it's over.

They're both busy and independent. They appreciate that in each other because they both need freedom to move around without having to account for every minute. He likes the way she's ready to go anywhere or do anything. At every opportunity, they're off to hike a new trail, go on a bike ride, or cross-country ski. They both crave new experiences and don't let details get in the way.

They have fun watching sports and reality shows on TV—anything that's fast-paced enough to keep their attention. Just add friends, beer, and pizza and it's a party!

He has a bossy side, but she doesn't take offense. If she doesn't like his ideas, she doesn't make a big deal out of it; she just goes about her business and does things her way.

The one thing she might change about him is the way he's focused on his little world, and doesn't think much about politics or the other big questions. When it comes to choosing between CNN or ESPN, there's no debate, at least not without a fight.

with a Taurus:

A Sagittarius woman often makes the first move with a Taurus man because he's kind of shy and she isn't. He's cute and she likes the way he speaks so directly; she gets the feeling she can trust him. Naturally, he's attracted to this interesting, funny woman who seems to find him interesting, too. So goes the dance of romance—and the agony of defeat.

The Sagittarius woman's motto is "Don't fence me in," and a Taurus man has a flowered plaque on the wall that reads, "Home, Sweet Home." That's the first clue they were not meant for each other. It won't be the last.

There was the time she labored in the kitchen for hours to prepare an authentic Indian dinner. He ate it to be nice, but he doesn't like exotic food and she could tell he wasn't thrilled. Some fun.

Then there are their different personalities. She needs a lot of stimulation—people, activities, places to go. She never feels more alive than when she's active. Boredom and depression can make her physically ill.

He wonders why she can't just stay busy at home. It must have been a Taurus-type old geezer who said, "When I works, I works hard, when I eats, I eats fast, and when I sits, I falls asleep." It's enough to drive a woman mad.

No, she won't have many rollicking good times with the Bull; no cavorting on the beach, no chopper rides, few, if any, exotic vacations. When even the security he brings to her life begins to feel like prison, it's time for her to move on.

with a Gemini:

The kind of casual companionship a Gemini man prefers feels right to a Sagittarius woman. She needs a man who lets her be herself and doesn't want to make her over into someone else. He keeps things light. For instance, he won't force her to change her life for him or make her promise total loyalty. He just wants to enjoy what they have today and not worry about tomorrow. That's fine with her, unless she's at the place in her life where she wants to settle down. But that's not often with a Saj, even a female Saj.

They have a great time watching movies (they like comedies) and they share an interest in books and conversation. They laugh at each other, themselves, their friends. They love to go on vacations together and if he travels for his job, she happily keeps her bag packed and gets time off, if possible.

The Sagittarian female has enthusiasm and energy for two women. She's curious about everything so whatever he's interested in, she'll happily throw herself into it wholeheartedly.

He doesn't have to share all her interests to be a fun friend and companion. For one thing, she's complex and interested in many subjects that might not be on his radar screen. He's happy to just keep moving and taking life as it comes. That's the beauty of not having to deal with all the adjustments marriage brings.

with a Cancer:

It's hard to imagine a Sagittarius woman staying in one place long enough to get something going with a Cancer man, unless it's at work. He doesn't come on strong and get her attention; rather, he has his own careful but slow approach to dating and mating.

Anyway, if they do hook up and get along great, he's ready to take the next logical step. In the Crab's worldview, people fall in love and they get married—that's the way it is. A Sagittarius woman might truly love him and even want a lasting relationship, but she may not want to have the wedding and everything that goes with it, especially if she's already had one failed marriage. This could be a serious problem for them and one that might not be fixable.

Another one: she goes about life in her busy cheerful way, but he's moody and quiet. Maybe he was offended by someone or had a bad day and he's looking for encouragement and tender words. She's not indifferent to his needs, but he doesn't speak up. Some might call her insensitive, but she's not callous; she just doesn't live on that feeling level. It's a difference in basic personalities.

If they do marry, there will be adjustments required by . . . guess who? She'll try to be more thoughtful, but she's still her own, independent self. He will be less sensitive later on when they've been together longer, but he still wants to do most things together.

with a Leo:

What happens when a loyal sign who needs a faithful mate like Leo meets up with a sign who needs a lot of freedom, like Sagittarius? Easy, if the Saj is a woman! She doesn't have to be promiscuous to enjoy life and have a great time; she just needs challenge, adventures, and a lot of laughs and she's the perfect, loyal partner for a Leo man!

They both want the finer things in life—good food, quality clothes, fine wine. If they're married, they enjoy their home and love to entertain. If they're just dating, they really get to express their fun-loving sides. This is the legendary whirlwind romance of song and story.

She has energy to spare. She can work full time, care for a house and children, and still happily shower him with attention and make him feel special—just what the big guy needs. If he tells her that he loves her and buys her extravagant gifts on their special occasions, she's one happy lady.

The Saj woman often uses humor to make a point, but she has to be careful to watch her sarcasm with a Leo, because some of her comments may not be taken in the spirit in which they were intended. That is, unless they use outrageous insults to playfully vent their irritation, like some couples.

In time, they learn what adjustments they must make to be happy. If big problems arise, they have a better chance of working things out than some sign combinations. At least their personalities complement one another.

with a Virgo:

The only reason a Sagittarius woman falls for a Virgo man is her eternal optimism. How do they differ? Let us count the ways.

In the beginning all is well, as usual. Her busy brain never slows down, so she's attracted to a Virgo man who is so obviously smart. He engages her with all kinds of ideas that keep her interested.

Eventually their different personality styles begin to grate on each other's nerves. She's a born entertainer who tends to exaggerate, so her stories are, shall we say, *mostly* true? Fortunately for her (perhaps not for the story), her Virgo lover is right there to point out each and every fuzzy fact.

A Sagittarius woman is not famous for moderation. She lives big and hates stingy portions of anything, especially delicious food. In spite of her activity, she can sometimes put on the pounds. Living with a Virgo man and listening to his cutting remarks about her weight won't help. Even though she laughs it off, it hurts more than she lets on.

More ways: she isn't good at making do or doing without, things a Virgo man takes satisfaction in. He thinks she spends way too much and she thinks he's too penny-pinching.

She does not keep a perfect house, nor does she care. He prefers it picked up and hopefully, clean. They could provide a balance for each other, but too often they just clash. After all, when a pendulum swings from one extreme to the other, it never stops in the middle.

with a Libra:

At last, a man with the tact to say, "No, honey, you look great in those pants and I love every inch of you." Enter the Libra man, with his pleasant personality and the way he refuses to make waves that he may have to calm later.

These are two "people" people who enjoy a good party or any excuse to get out and have a good time. They have their differences, but mostly they don't amount to much and they add dimension to their union.

She's a little louder and more extroverted than he is, and doesn't care if people agree with her opinions, which she states for all to hear. He's more tactful, perhaps more polished, than she. It's like he thinks life is a popularity contest and you have to *make nice* to win. Sometimes it is, but she won't win any awards for diplomacy herself, and that's OK with her. She's so funny and entertaining, people enjoy being around her. Think *The Unsinkable Molly Brown* and those highbrows who grew to love her.

If they decorate a home together it will be eclectic and interesting. His tastes lean toward the harmonic, well-balanced, and color-coordinated, minimalist look. She likes bright, even outlandish color schemes, unique wall treatments, over-sized furniture, and at least one wall where she can display her collection of curios from all over the world.

They dress in most dissimilar fashions. He is neatly turned out and conservatively attired, she's in multiple colors and interesting combinations. She dresses like she lives, with a flair and style all her own. So does he, nothing eye-catching, but nothing that can be criticized, either. Bottom line for these two: not bad, not bad at all.

with a Scorpio:

A Sagittarius woman has a funny, sarcastic personality that attracts a Scorpio man with his dry sense of humor. But when she has everyone else laughing hysterically, he looks on with a sardonic smile. He never shows his feelings, while she's just the opposite, outgoing and friendly. That's one reason why these two make strange bedfellows as well as friends.

He has secrets that he never reveals. That's the double-secret part. Everything else in his life, including if he had measles as a child, is his business, and not to be mentioned except by him, if he chooses. Now everyone knows a Sagittarius woman never *could* keep a secret; that's why she doesn't have any—her life is an open book. If that's true, then his life must be a small piece of paper covered with tiny hieroglyphics, folded up and squirreled away in his wallet. How is she going to remember what she can and cannot mention? How is he going to forgive her when she blabs his business to her friends?

His jealousy is too confining for her to cope with. If he's one of those Scorpios who thinks she belongs to him (yes, there are still some of them out there) and if he makes the mistake of telling her, well, hell hath no fury . . . . Even before feminism, a Sagittarius woman wouldn't have any part of that!

They can have a fine romp in the hay, but as soon as they get the straw out of their hair, they'd best go their separate ways. Trust me.

with another Sagittarius:

Let the games begin! These two aren't looking for domestic bliss as much as adventure together. There are many roads these two might wander down, different lifestyles they can adopt. But whatever they choose, or serendipitously fall into, there will be certain recurring themes.

The first is travel. Either or both may travel for work. Or travel may *be* their work. Short of that, they will spend a lot of money on vacations; to them, it isn't a vacation unless they get out of town and, preferably, out of the country. Here is one couple who doesn't equate marriage with settling down.

The second necessity is learning—through classes, reading, TV, travel, or discussion. They each work out a philosophy they can live with concerning spiritual issues and the big questions in life. They could be perennial students or inspiring teachers and happily embrace a life in academia. If they're not inclined toward that, they will still have knowledgeable opinions on many topics.

Number three is getting outdoors. They might own a little land with some animals, or a sports-oriented business. They might lead river-running expeditions or teach skiing. Or they may just enjoy walks, hikes, and gardening—anything to be outside in the wide open spaces that they love.

If they have a business together, it will either be a rousing success or a big flop because they don't understand moderation. They're high-energy folks who don't have time for petty concerns. Everything is big, including their fights, but they'll forgive each other magnanimously in the end and have a great making-up party.

with a Capricorn:

Think of this couple as a clown in a red fright wig in love with a duke . . . a rodeo queen with an accountant . . . a gypsy with a minister. Only Cupid or love or chemistry would pair these two because no rational person would.

She needs lots of room to spread out and move around. He likes his house like his mind, organized and orderly.

Her idea of an ideal partner is someone who likes to laugh and have a good time, go places, and who asks bigger questions than, "Did you buy plenty of beer?"

He thinks in the long term and plans for the future. She believes the future will take care of itself, and anyway, why worry? It isn't even here yet. Even if she tries to be practical, her indomitable, irrepressible spirit will trump her best intentions, and she's likely to dump both the budget and the schedule for a new and exciting possibility.

Yes, she wants a comfortable home and security like any woman, but the difference between her and other signs is that she's not willing to give up anything she wants to do for mere things.

She can get out-of-sorts, or, let's face it, damn grumpy if she's bored or restless, and his tendency to work long hours, and even weekends, will wear on her after so long.

A Capricorn man who sometimes walks around with a black cloud over his head and a Sagittarius woman who is easygoing and upbeat are going to have their challenges. Can love conquer all? Has it ever? More to the point, is it likely?

with an Aquarius:

If these two invited all their friends to one party, they'd have to rent a hall! They collect people like some folks collect coins or stamps. Some of her friends are poor, some wealthy, some even famous. All are well-loved by her. Some of his friends are oddballs, some are in science or the arts, some even in jail. All are his lifelong friends.

These two hit it off from their first meeting and will probably always remain pals. Here is a guy who is interested in everything like she is. They can talk for hours, comparing opinions, swapping tales, sharing ideas. One thing she needs in a relationship is a lot of intellectual stimulation. There are a dozen subjects she's interested in, but hasn't had time to explore.

He's willing to give her the breathing space she needs, and that's a good thing, because she already had a busy life when she met him. She doesn't pressure him either, so they know when they *do* see each other, it's because they both want to.

They probably share an interest in a cause they both believe in. They might work together on animal rights, for instance, or protecting the environment, possibly a civic cause of some type. They are both natural crusaders who fight for the underdog.

Both are willing to go wherever life takes them, as long as they can explore a new horizon or begin a new venture. If they could glimpse the future, and who says they can't, maybe they would see themselves somewhere down the road a far piece, holding hands.

with a Pisces:

The tarot card reader told her she would meet a man who would play an important role in her life, but to be careful because she could get hurt. Then she met a Pisces man, right on schedule. Of course, she threw caution to the winds and went for it. No matter what anyone might say, even a psychic, if a Sagittarius woman wants something, no one will talk her out of it.

At first, naturally, he's lovely. He's interested in her projects, he's kind to people and animals, and he's a wonderful, romantic, thoughtful lover. He makes her laugh and what's better than that?

Ideally she has a Pisces man who is genuine and not playing a role, because she isn't good at detecting insincerity or phoniness. She believes in people and assumes they are who they say they are. Hopefully he doesn't have some tragic event in his past that keeps him from having a healthy relationship with a woman.

Some Pisces men are dreamers who won't or can't stay with one job. If she has this type of Fish look out, because a Sagittarius woman can be too generous for her own good. She won't think twice about loaning him money or buying him things. But as generous as she is, she hates to be taken advantage of. She will figure it out if he's a user. A Sagittarius woman is *not* the victim type.

Was she careful, as advised to be? No. Was she hurt? Yes, but she has a happy heart that will survive to love another day.

The Capricorn Woman

December 22–January 19

The Capricorn girl was a serious youngster with a quiet confidence and a desire to please her parents. She did well in school and grasped new concepts with ease. She was a leader with her friends and liked to act as teacher to younger kids. She didn't play a lot with dolls—she was either a tomboy or a glamour queen. She had high aspirations for her life and was eager to know about everything in the world so she could figure out what to set her sights on.

She wasn't quite accepted in school: her family moved a lot or they were of a different religion or culture. Sometimes she felt unaccepted in her own family because of divorce or illness. Perhaps because of her own loneliness, she was compassionate with the classmate who was teased or ridiculed.

Her relationship with her father was strained for reasons that were not her fault. She may have had a crush on an older family friend or teacher who was a substitute father figure. Her strong drive to succeed became a way to prove that she does, indeed, belong.

She happily did favors for elderly neighbors and enjoyed talking to them as equals. She was reserved in expressing her feelings; she loved her pets because she could open up emotionally to them.

As a teen, she didn't require constant supervision. She had the common sense to make good decisions most of the time and act as her own parent. She wasn't dependent on the approval of her peers because she already had an idea of where she wanted her life to go. She had worries and self-doubts, but they only made her more determined to succeed.

She valued higher education for the knowledge, of course, but her main goal was the degree that would open doors for her. Regardless of where she began her career, she will finish at, or near, the top.

Although she was a romantic and may have had several affairs, when it came to choosing a life partner, she judged men against her mental list of "Qualities I Want in a Husband." If the Las Vegas "Little Chapel in the Glen" depended on Capricorn women, they'd be out of business. She feels secure in an old-fashioned marriage and she makes her husband the head of the household—although he rules, like a presidential appointee, at her pleasure.

If she has a career, she brings home the bacon—fries it up in a pan—and never forgets she's a feminine creature at heart. If she's a stay-at-home mom, she firmly runs an organized household and her children don't get away with much. She is one of the few who can successfully home-school her children. She's an excellent role model with her persistence, courage, and love. She helps her husband succeed with her wise counsel and encouragement.

She is well into her thirties before she molds her life to her satisfaction. As time goes by, she just keeps getting better and smarter. She doesn't peak until middle age—or even later, seeming to get younger as she ages, and less serious. She accepts herself as she becomes more accepting of people and their different ways.

As a mature woman, she has developed wisdom and depth. She has fought courageously against depression, health problems, and relationship challenges. When she looks back and sees all the things she's triumphed over, she finally gives herself the credit she deserves.

The Capricorn woman in love . . .

with an Aries:

In spite of his "Aren't I great?" attitude, an Aries man is just a little boy trying to prove himself, so a strong Capricorn woman can scare him off if she isn't careful. She learned long ago to soften her approach so as not to threaten a man's ego. If he's pursuing a plan she thinks is doomed to fail, she quietly, but confidently, helps him make a better decision. He sometimes even takes her advice. They make an excellent team in business with his optimism and her common sense, but they need separate areas of responsibility.

In a romantic relationship, it's a little trickier. She lets him know she loves and admires him, but they still have conflicting opinions. They both must be willing to negotiate and compromise, but an Aries man wants to do things his way and he doesn't like his motives or methods questioned. If they can manage to work out the kinks, each can bring something to the relationship that benefits the other. She can learn to relax and have more fun, and he can learn to be more organized.

She's more work-oriented than he is and probably won't take time off to accompany him on some of his recreational trips. If she's okay with him going with his friends, he won't mind going without her.

Lucky is the Aries man who has a capable, down-to-earth Capricorn woman to keep him grounded. But will he appreciate it? That's the question.

with a Taurus:

A Taurus man is hard-working like a Capricorn woman, and just as practical, but no one works all the time. When she wants to relax and enjoy an evening out, she likes to go to an elegant restaurant, eat well, and enjoy an excellent glass of wine. She likes quality in all things, but he prefers a place where the food is like home-cooking and the dress code is, well, there isn't one. They can take turns choosing the restaurant, but she won't be happy going out with a man who doesn't look respectable. It won't take her long to get him out of that old T-shirt and faded jeans. He might never have her sense of style, but she'll get him looking presentable, at least when they're out together.

He won't light any cozy fires unless he's cold, or whisk her away for a romantic weekend unless it's part of a business trip. But they get along pretty well. They both honor their commitments. If he says he'll do something, he does it and vice versa.

Some men see her devotion to her work as a threat to their egos, but a Taurus man respects her commitment and admires her ambition. He's happy to know his rival is a job, not another guy. And anyway, he's a peaceful sort and not inclined to pick a fight. As long as she leaves dinner in the fridge, he's content. If he's well-fed and secure, he's even happy for the occasional opportunity to be alone and in total charge of the remote.

These two have a solid foundation for their future just by doing what comes naturally. They may not hit any peaks of passion, but neither will they slog through the valley of bankruptcy, and that's huge.

with a Gemini:

With a Capricorn woman, a Gemini man must face up to the fact that he's got a no-nonsense woman, just in case he was thinking of trying any.

He takes things lightly and she takes things seriously: that about sums it up for this duo—many differences of style here. For instance, when she brings up the subject of IRAs and savings accounts, his eyes glaze over and she knows she's been tuned out. With a Gemini man, she better get used to handling these things herself, which is better anyway because she consults experts for financial advice and he asks his brother or neighbor.

Travel is a different experience for these two signs. He loves spur-of-the-moment trips, while she wants to plan well in advance. His thoughts are of the interesting people and places they will see, while she is making sure it fits into their budget and planning what to pack. He can change his mind about where to go while she's out shopping for the right clothes. It can be exasperating for both of them.

Her life goals are all about working hard and getting ahead. He hasn't planned anything past Thursday. When he quits yet another job, he'll give her forty reasons why it was necessary. But eventually his flip-flopping and inability to stay focused on one thing will have her on anti-depressants.

If they stick together, she may eventually help him become less irresponsible. And he can help her become more spontaneous and light-hearted. That and world peace—all these are possibilities. More likely scenario: he strays, she divorces him, she gets the house.

with a Cancer:

Although these two are opposites in many ways, their relationship can succeed if they don't give up too soon because they have some things in common. They both value financial security; if they do get into difficulties, they will go to credit counseling to get back on track.

They both look forward to remodeling and improving their house, which they fill with inherited antiques and family photos. The challenge is their different temperaments.

A Cancer man lives with his emotions on his sleeve, while a Capricorn woman is matter-of-fact. She proves her love by getting married, working hard for their future, and raising a family with him. He needs more reassurance than that. He wants to hear how happy he makes her and what she appreciates about him. Alas, it doesn't come naturally to the strong-minded Capricorn woman; she's not that kind of gal. She expects everyone to be independent (like her) and just get the job done.

Her career will always be important to her. It adds to his anxiety if she spends *too* much time away, or he perceives her as *too* dedicated to her job.

If they are aware of these differences in temperament, they can learn to accept each other as is. She can learn to be more tender and reassuring *some* of the time and he can realize that her down-to-earth, plain-speaking ways don't mean for a minute she doesn't love him.

If and when children come along, they will grow up in a secure environment with college paid for. There may not be many wild and crazy times in this family, but there won't be any nasty surprises, either.

with a Leo:

Even if she's unloaded the dishwasher a thousand times, she must be ready with a "Good job, thank you so very, very much!" if he does it once. Yes, it irks, but there it is! This guy has to be treated with respect and love, being the king and all. If she can remember this, they have a chance. She must think he's worth it, or she won't give it that much effort.

She has a down-to-earth approach to life and love, and he needs a fan club. It's similar to the problems she has with a Cancer man, except a Leo man needs even more appreciation for his acts of thoughtfulness and his accomplishments. Will she give him the applause and recognition he needs? She will if she wants to. When he's content in his marriage, a Leo man is very encouraging; in fact, he enjoys helping others—it reinforces his superiority. But she should still be prepared to do most of the giving.

Another source of problems is their differing approaches to money. She wants to buy an IRA or at least get the bills paid off. He wants to do that too, except that he just saw a $3,000 plasma TV that would be so great-looking in the family room! He wants only the best, feels he deserves it, and that's what he buys. So does she, but only if and when they can afford it.

with a Virgo:

Finally! A man who doesn't complain that she works too much! Virgo is a good sign for a Capricorn woman. They're both hard-working and committed to their jobs. Of the two, however, the Capricorn woman is more ambitious. Although a Virgo man judges himself on how he performs at work, he doesn't necessarily have his eye on moving up. He prefers to do what he knows and do it well.

She's the one who has her eye on the next career step. If one of them has to give up a job so a partner can take advantage of a promotion and transfer to another state, it's probably him. When children come along, they will be looking for a good nanny.

Even so, she defers to his good judgment at times. Although she doesn't like to take direction from anyone, she admits that sometimes his ideas are just as practical as hers.

This relationship can work for the Capricorn woman if she doesn't have too many expectations. She must stay away from romance novels; they only make her aware of what she doesn't have with a Virgo man—in a word, romance. (She doesn't read them, anyway.) If she can accept him for what he is, a hard-working, no-frills, down-to-earth guy, they have a chance. There will be few fights about money and he'll probably want her to handle the bills. Since financial security is one of her basic needs, she's happy to oblige.

with a Libra:

Both Libra and Capricorn admire the finer things in life and the luxuries money can buy. They both opt for quality over quantity, but there the similarity ends.

She believes anything worth having is worth working for, while the Libra male believes that good things come to those who ask—or know how to play the angles. She doesn't respect a man who wants something for nothing. She works hard to feel she deserves what she gets, so this attitude irritates her to no end.

The weekends go something like this: she's busy doing laundry, cooking, and putting next week's meals in the freezer. He's busy watching sports. She doesn't realize he maintains his balance by working hard and then doing absolutely nothing to make up for it. If she asks him to fix the lawn mower, he murmurs, "Okay, honey," and then never does it.

He's pleasant to have around, and that's what appealed to her about him in the first place, but it can be a difficult relationship. They both want to take the lead, but he does it in a more diplomatic way, i.e., he says what he knows she wants to hear, and then proceeds to do it his way. She takes the direct approach and tells it like it is. She's disillusioned when she realizes he doesn't always mean what he says.

If he was looking for someone to help him make decisions, she's right there. With her wisdom and common sense, she comes up with the best approach every time.

with a Scorpio:

The Capricorn woman thinks she can figure anything out logically. Then she meets this fascinating Scorpio man! He's intriguing, exciting, and mysterious. He doesn't follow any of the rules she's set down for relationships, so he keeps her a little off-balance, a feeling she's not used to.

These are two signs that don't have any glaring differences; just a difference in outlook. They are both loyal and believe in true love, but she may find out that his idea of being true is different from hers. He is true to her in his own way, which means mentally, not necessarily physically. He likes to have a secret life, or friend, or something, which no one else knows about. It's this *secrecy* thing he has.

They both want to achieve success and power, but success is more important to her, while power is his ultimate goal. He thinks he retains an edge if people don't know everything about him or what he's thinking. A man like that isn't easy to get close to. She makes decisions based on the information she has, and if he doesn't let her in on his inner thoughts and feelings, he has an advantage. Unfortunately, that's the game he plays.

This straightforward woman will never understand a Scorpio man. He has hidden emotional depths that she will never fathom, and in spite of her remarkable managerial abilities, she'll never be able to mold this guy into anything but what he already is. For a Capricorn woman, is that fair?

with a Sagittarius:

He doesn't want to be the head of the household—he just wants to be a regular guy with few responsibilities, so he's happy to let her make the major decisions. That solves one problem.

They could run a business together and be an awesome team. But living together in an intimate relationship is harder to navigate successfully. His outlook on life seems unrealistic to her—he certainly isn't grounded in reality like she is. He might have been fun and exciting when they were dating, but his casual attitude begins to wear on her eventually. After all, she wants children, and that means she needs someone she can count on. She wants financial security and that means watching the budget.

His charisma blinded her at first. He wants to have fun and experience life to the fullest! He doesn't think about his bank balance if a friend calls and invites him to go on a hiking trip in the Grand Canyon. He takes the time off, even if it's without pay.

Even when he works, he finds a way to make it exciting. He tries to make sure his job includes travel, if possible. There's nothing that gets his juices running like seeing something for the first time. She wants to conserve and save, to work first and play later.

Another stumbling block might be their religious outlooks. While the Sagittarian man has a broad comprehension of spirituality, the Capricorn woman may stick to the traditional religion of her family.

This possible twosome seems impossible. They should give it up before they're in too deep, or make sure their insurance covers marriage counseling.

with another Capricorn:

Two Capricorns can share the values of working hard, saving for the future, and being loyal to the family. They raise their children to be conscientious like themselves and expect them to work for their allowances. They take them to church and raise them to be solid citizens.

If their children are little Geminis or Sagittarians or Librans, there will be struggles and a certain amount of family upheaval when the kids get older and begin to break away from the strict (and to them, restrictive) rules they have grown up with.

Both Capricorns probably came from a good family background, because that's important to them in a mate. They will have many beautiful antiques inherited from their respective families. They like tradition and they value the heritage of the past. They carefully hang the beloved decorations on their Christmas tree that have been handed down for generations.

One small glitch. A Capricorn man is the boss at work and it can carry over into his home life. For instance, he doesn't know more about investing and finances than she does, he just *thinks* he does. He might say, "This is what we should do," forgetting her competence and creating tension between them.

The two of them need to make a real effort to build fun and relaxation into their lives—in other words, lighten up. Their kids will help them be conscious of that. Setting aside a day each week or so for a "date" is a good idea. They need the time alone to keep their relationship healthy.

with an Aquarius:

Now here is an interesting combo. Not good, but interesting. She likes to know what to expect and he likes to do the unexpected. Obviously, this is a match made in heaven by someone with a sense of humor.

Take a simple thing like choosing where to eat. He wants to try that new sushi place he heard about at work. She wants to go to one of her favorite restaurants, where she knows just what to order and that she will enjoy it.

After the initial fun of dating is over, she wants to settle down to domestic happiness. Just the words "settle down" make him uneasy. He doesn't want to be tied down, not now, not ever. He hates routine and will do something totally outrageous, sometimes just for shock value. This isn't a good match for serenity's sake.

His friends play an important part in his life, and marriage doesn't mean he won't still spend time with them. If he has them over to the house too much, she frowns on it. She likes family time and that means no company.

It's possible he will be gone a lot. His interests range far and wide and he is fascinated by whatever is new, anything from a religion to an invention to a place, and all points in between. He can seem remote because even when he's physically there, his mind is traveling to a zillion places. The Capricorn woman's seductive side blossoms only when she feels secure in a relationship. With an Aquarian man, that's a stretch!

with a Pisces:

A Capricorn woman may not be sensitive enough for a Pisces man. He thinks, "When she sees I'm lost, she will find a way to gently guide me back." She thinks, "Get a life!" She's a strong person and respects strength in others. Her business sense and shrewd judgment can help him in his career, but if he leans on her too much, she loses respect for him. She isn't one to express sympathy, so she seems uncaring and even cold sometimes. While she has profound depth of insight when she's being sensitive, sometimes she has to be reminded to imagine how her words sound to him.

If a couple can't come together on their money it can drive them apart, and the way these two approach finances is totally different. Money isn't the most important thing to him. It isn't to her, either, but it's near the top of the list. He feels sorry for every troubled soul he runs across. Good friend, distant relative, or a guy he met at the local bar—they all qualify as deserving to him and he wants to help them. Sometimes it's just advice or an encouraging word they need, but too often, it's cold, hard cash. She views many of his good causes with disdain, especially when he lends money to people who never pay it back. She doesn't feel sympathy for people who made poor choices. Soon he starts keeping it from her and that leads to a habit of evasion and lies.

If he is a Pisces with a good sense of himself, he will enjoy her competence. If not, he will be threatened and she will be turned off, and the union won't last, simple as that.

The Aquarius Woman

January 20–February 18

A tiny Aquarius seemed to be two different babies—docile and content at times but fussy and inconsolable at others. Her mother couldn't decide exactly what kind of baby . . . . That's the Aquarius girl—a little bundle of contradictions from heaven!

As a young girl, she collected friends and acquaintances of all description. She wasn't a follower, yet she needed her friends' approval. At other times, she happily spent hours alone, inventing games to satisfy her curiosity and imagination.

She looked up to her dad and identified more with him and his role than she did with the homemaking instincts of her mom. She wasn't as likely to have a real close friend like most little girls, instead preferring the company of boys. This pattern stayed with her as she matured, and she still feels more comfortable in a man's world.

At least once in her childhood, she had to re-create her world when the family moved to another state or something else unexpected happened. Changes occur throughout her life, but she always adjusts and goes on.

As a young woman, her parents were stunned when she rebelled against their teachings. She understood their views, but had her own ideas and didn't mind voicing her opinions. She hated rules that restricted her freedom, and she was already open-minded and accepting of alternate lifestyles. She may have experimented sexually or adopted a different religion to prove she would live her life her own way.

There was at least one occasion when she fell head-over-heels in love. The suddenness of it and her abandonment of caution made it memorable, indeed. She found she could ignore society's conventions with little remorse—she was used to feeling different, anyway.

Her life can take many paths as an adult because her unpredictability makes it impossible to generalize.

Her marriage is one of equality because she won't have it any other way. She is busily involved in her life as a wife and mother, volunteering at her children's school and probably also at church or in the community with any number of causes that benefit society. She handles her career with equal assurance. She shares her knowledge wherever it's needed.

She continues to have many friends, but few intimate ones. She's ahead of her time and is interested in whatever is new: technology, ideas, lifestyles, medical breakthroughs, people, and just about everything.

She has an odd sense of humor and some pretty off-the-wall ideas. When she's annoyed, she spits sarcasm but is so funny she makes people laugh.

As a mature woman, she's decided she likes her quirks and eccentricities. She has grown in self-confidence and inner serenity.

Finally, she will learn to take care of herself and not just do for everyone else. She will learn to express her emotions and be willing to be vulnerable by sharing her inner self. Most important, she will learn to ask for the affection and love she needs.

Her title is, "Most Likely to Do the Unlikely." She's interesting, unpredictable, and wants to leave the world a better place for having been here.

The Aquarius woman in love . . .

with an Aries:

An Aquarius woman is drawn to an Aries man more out of curiosity than anything, because domineering men are not her favorite. He can tell she isn't enthralled with him, and that piques his interest. She doesn't usually jump into anything, but if he catches her at just the right time in her life, she just may do it. With her it's difficult to predict.

She doesn't push for promises about the future, which is a relief to him. If he tries the macho stuff with her, she's turned off, but she's intrigued by his spontaneity—she gets bored with routine like he does. He says whatever he thinks and she likes that about him too.

Her life was already busy when she met him, and she isn't about to give up any of her interests. He may eventually feel she's ignoring him, or not putting him first—and that's hard for him to believe! He seems to want it both ways. He likes the way she doesn't need him to be there 100 percent of the time, but he wants to be number one with her. Still, he loves to do guy stuff with his friends on a regular basis, so that gives her ample opportunity to do her own thing.

She has friends of all ages and backgrounds and all walks of life. He has to understand this and not be threatened, which is easy for him. As long as he doesn't try to dominate her they have a pretty darn good chance. There's a good deal of give and take between them and that's the way she likes it.

with a Taurus:

The physical attraction is there, but these two cramp each other's style. For starters, she doesn't conform to any traditional women's role. Like Hillary, she isn't here to bake cookies and stand by her man. She needs a tolerant, understanding guy who doesn't come with pre-conceived ideas of what she should do. She can't be typed because she doesn't fit any mold.

He's a basically simple guy who doesn't need a fancy, complicated life. When she tries to change him or get him involved with her social causes, he digs in his heels and resists. The peaceful life he loves is monotonous to her. He lives in the here and now, and she's always thinking about the future. She has many friends and acquaintances and gets invitations for all kinds of fancy events and parties. He enjoys home life more than she does, but can be talked into going; she knows how.

He has a hard time adjusting to her unconventional ideas. When she goes off on a tangent without warning, it's hard for him to deal with. His behavior is predictable and he hates surprises. He'll never understand her and will have to make some concessions if they want to co-exist in a somewhat peaceful manner. She has to be crazy about him to put up with him.

They both hold fast to their opinions and think one another stubborn, which they are, but especially him. She, at least, will change her mind when more information comes in, but she's hard to convince based on his opinion only. If these two find they aren't compatible, she will be the one to end it.

with a Gemini:

For an Aquarian woman, love begins with companionship and that's fine with him, so their romance begins as two friends having fun. She's attracted to his mind more than his body and he enjoys an interesting woman, so they're off to a good start. They both enjoy mental games and trivia. She knows who won Academy Awards last year and who the actress was who played opposite Tom Hanks in *Big*. He can recall who played in the Superbowl for the last ten years and who invented the personal computer. They both have low boredom quotients so they will find all kinds of things to do, social events, movies, lectures, evenings spent playing games with friends. They enjoy sharing their music and books.

They are compatible, but they can also get on each other's nerves; it's impossible to predict with these two. Because she's quite a bit wiser in a subconscious, spiritual sense than he is, she will be the most tolerant and the most giving when they argue, unless he distorts the truth—then she's outraged.

If she cries when they fight, he doesn't respond with tender words. He's more likely to leave, or stay and make things worse by seeming to be indifferent to her pain. He's not, he just can't stand emotional scenes.

They will probably go together for a long time before they decide to marry. If they never get around to it, they will remain friends and that's probably a better deal for them anyway—it takes less courage and faith. If they do marry, they can usually overcome their disagreements with a little extra goodwill and negotiation.

with a Cancer:

A woman shouldn't really take up with a man she wants to change. And yet, that's the very thing that happens with a Cancer man and an Aquarius woman.

She gets along with someone who gives her space and won't complain if she's busy and often away from home. He wants to be with her, but he hates being dragged out to all her functions. He can sulk if he has to make his own dinner and dine alone too often, or at all.

He likes knowing what to expect, so it's hard on his sense of security when she springs surprises on him, like when she quit her job and decided to go into sales. Or when she announced she was going to start teaching a yoga class on Tuesday nights. "At least," he thinks, "she could have asked me first." She does her best to be considerate unless she's too busy and preoccupied to notice.

Like him, she likes to accumulate things—not because she's sentimental or a pack rat like he is, but because they strike her fancy.

This is a difficult relationship with little chance of success, but still a chance. If she knows what role she plays in perpetuating their problems, she might change her attitude toward him and start the healing process. If he is a Crab with a good sense of humor, that helps, but he has to take a deep breath and let her go in order to keep her. In the end, they both want the same things; they just have different personalities and ways of going after them.

with a Leo:

An Aquarius woman knows a man is right for her if she feels totally loved by him when she is being entirely herself, because she won't pretend to be something she is not.

A Leo man won't ridicule her ideas or what she believes. That doesn't mean he won't have his private opinion. But with his live-and-let-live attitude, he has no need to prove someone else wrong, as long as he's the kind of Lion who's secure in himself.

If she's into astrology, for instance, he listens while she reads the compatibility chart she printed for them off the Internet. With a touch of condescension in his tone, he remarks on how well it fits them, even if he doesn't agree for a minute when it mentions his need for recognition.

There are some things they have to work on, however. She believes in the absolute equality of the sexes, so naturally it irritates her when he thinks he can decide which restaurant they go to, for example, or when they should take their vacation. A Leo man always thinks his desires and needs supercede anyone else's. But she doesn't meekly let him have his way. She might use some unusual methods to make it fair, like inventing a complicated schedule for who chooses what, when.

If she runs off to a meeting and he's left to fend for himself, he can get quite huffy and annoyed, which is, in itself, annoying.

He might eventually learn to be more detached and independent like her, and she might adopt some of his optimism. But that's after years of marriage have softened them up.

with a Virgo:

The Virgo man wants to have everything organized and all his books in a row. The Aquarian woman is energized by chaos and is too busy to keep an immaculate house. The way they live indicates the way their minds work, so these signs present a definite relationship challenge. They should study one another, preferably at a distance, before they ever become more than casual lovers.

He never forgets a face, a name, a date, or an address. He frets and analyzes and plans his next move. She has a sort of mental fuzziness

with a Sagittarius:

An Aquarian woman doesn't need to possess her man and a Sagittarius man wouldn't let her anyway, so no harm, no foul. They are equals and give each other the space to be themselves. Neither is especially impressed by money or prestige and they both enjoy people from all backgrounds. But when they develop an intimate relationship, they generate sparks and then their cozy fire can become a firestorm. He isn't usually bossy or domineering, he just likes to have his own way, but she doesn't like to be talked into things. Amazingly, they can usually get over it with little or no bitterness.

He lives for adventure and she's up for anything new and different. They both have many goals and many things they want to accomplish. They share a curiosity about the world, its inhabitants, and all the oddities therein. She has a more intellectual way of exploring and he, a more physical. On vacation ... e might be deep into a book about hands-on healing or the Kabala. They are both able to give the other some space and that's important.

When he, being his usual tactless self, blusters and exaggerates, she can usually ignore his comments and not take them to heart. As far as her little idiosyncrasies, sure, she's bizarre at times, but her eccentric behavior, rather than startling him or putting him off, is likely to entertain him.

She has oodles of friends and hopefully he likes them, because if he doesn't, he tells her so. She chuckles in amusement as she picks up the phone to invite them over for lunch.

with a Capricorn:

To say that a Capricorn man is more conventional than an Aquarius woman is like saying Bush is more Republican than Clinton. She searches for what's right for her and to heck with other people's opinions. She believes in the truth, same as him, but it's her own personal interpretation of it. She does, however, respect a man who holds true to his principles, even if she doesn't agree with them.

She works right beside him if they have their own business and willingly trains for whatever job is needed. But when they try to make decisions jointly, they run into problems. He wants things done his way, but she won't budge in her opinions. And yet, if anyone is to change, it will probably be her, since Capricorn men are set in their ways from early on. But she can't be forced; she has to make up her own mind.

She comes up with new methods and different ways of doing things. Not so with him. He is uncomfortable with anything that hasn't stood the test of time and wants to do things the same way his father did.

Their social life and what they like to do is different for each. She likes any occasion to mingle with a group and if it's for a good cause, all the better. He isn't comfortable in a room full of people he doesn't know. He enjoys his comfortable rut and doesn't want anyone to drag him out of it.

Even though they are different personalities entirely, their differences can work for them if they communicate and both are willing to make concessions.

with another Aquarius:
A man of any other sign is going to think she has way too many friends—only he can appreciate what they mean to her. They are both more comfortable with a friend than a lover; it's less confining. A pair of Aquarians can be close, platonic friends for a long time before their relationship progresses to the romance stage.

When they do marry, they have hundreds to invite to the wedding, including her ex and his family and his ex and their kids. Confused? It takes an Aquarian to keep everyone straight and get along with them all to boot.

They want to get married on top of a mountain, on a ship, or some other odd place. At the least, there will be something that makes their wedding unique.

Just because they have the same Sun sign, they don't see eye-to-eye on everything. If they disagree whether to make the living room into an office or paint the bedroom fuchsia, they come up with a unique way to decide the issue—maybe rock, paper, scissors.

Their household can be a disorganized mess because they have so many irons in the fire. When they compare day planners, they see it's impossible to keep all their commitments. At Christmas, they need at least four boxes of cards, not that they ever get around to sending them out.

How a relationship between two Aquarians will turn out is anyone's guess, since they never do the expected. One risk is it's hard to keep romance alive when the kitchen is always crowded with people. For another, they may see so much of each other's friends that either he or she becomes attracted to one of them.

with a Pisces:

a rich imagination and life can help an Aquarian woman act out her bedroom fantasies as anything from the friendly plumber to a secret agent. Now if only he plays his real self the rest of the time. The average Pisces man doesn't usually intentionally disguise who he is, although some certainly do. But he's so inconsistent, he could become someone else next month or next year.

He is attracted by her unconventionality and she is intrigued by his humor and willingness to make fun of himself. They get along famously at first, but any hint of disloyalty or dishonesty that she sees turns her off.

If he's one of those Fish who doesn't know how to acquire financial security or even land a well-paying job, she forgives his limitations and willingly provides assistance in any way she can. But if he continually gives his money or things away to whatever person or cause he thinks needs them more, she gets fed up. When her savings is exhausted, so is her patience.

There are as many Pisces "types" as there are fish in the aquarium, so their relationship can range far and wide and so can their magic together. It can have a spiritual base, in which case, they will help each other reach new heights. Or they may have a mutual purpose that they pursue together to make the world a better place.

They can find happiness, but they can also find disenchantment. They will both put up with only so much pain from the other before she breaks up with him, or he drifts away from her.

THE PISCES WOMAN
FEBRUARY 19—MARCH 20

A Pisces girl is a rare gift of a daughter—feminine, obedient, and sweet. She can be happy by herself for hours, especially if given all variety of materials for crafts and art. Her rich imagination comes up with the most extraordinary creations. Later, reading is an escape for her and she especially loves stories of fantasy and magic where elves, gnomes, fairies, and all sorts of supernatural beings exist in other-worldly places. Starting with *Alice in Wonderland* and continuing on through *The Lord of the Rings* and romance novels, her heart feels at home in fantasy landscapes, oftentimes more than in the real world.

She isn't sure what she wants to be when she grows up. She isn't even sure who she'd rather play with or what she wants to do. She lets her friends take the lead and is content to follow along. When they play at fairy tales, she doesn't have to be Cinderella; she can play the part of the Prince, or even the stepmother. Her truest role would be the compassionate Fairy Godmother, because even a young Pisces wants to help someone in need.

There is usually some tragic overlay in a Pisces girl's existence, either something that happens to her or someone close to her that permanently shades her perception of life. She might be ill-treated in some way, either by a parent, a relative, or her environment, either or all of which fail to protect her. She understands that sadness is part of life and perhaps that is why she unconsciously reaches for the happily-ever-after aspect of fantasy.

The typical Pisces teenager is hard to describe, since she is different with different people and she changes, depending on her environment. As a teen, she isn't sure what kind of boy is right for her. She only knows she needs love and acceptance, and she sets out to search for it, sometimes looking where she is least likely to find it. It seems she has a knack for choosing the wrong man, as if being hurt is inevitable. Since she isn't sure of her own worth and needs someone to affirm it, she becomes dependent and sometimes accepts mistreatment.

She's tender enough to be moved to tears at the birth of a baby or at the beauty of a snow-covered peak, but when trouble comes along, she surprises even herself with her strength. As a mature woman, she has often married more than once or at least has had several serious relationships, whether consummated or not. She's proved to be a survivor by taking the hard knocks and learning some difficult lessons, like how not to give her power away to another person and that she is strong enough to take care of herself.

She has the empathy to feel what another is feeling and her natural instinct has always been to help a troubled friend. But she has realized that negativity affects her deeply, so whenever possible, she surrounds herself with cheerful, optimistic people.

She has learned to love herself and not always put everyone's needs ahead of her own—that it's healthy to be a little selfish. Now that she doesn't *need* it, she is ready for the relationship of which she has been dreaming.

The Pisces woman in love . . .

with an Aries:

An Aries man can engulf a Pisces woman with his forceful and electrifying personality. If she is at the stage where she isn't sure of what she wants, his very strength and decisiveness are comforting. And yet, there were never two people so different.

She sees life as a mystery unfolding; a series of connected events and complicated relationships. If he can't see it, he doesn't think about it, so the unknowable has no meaning for him. He is in pursuit of his personal goals and adventures. And yet, there is a certain rightness to this relationship, his being such a masculine sign and hers, so feminine. In that way, they are perfect for each other, like Romeo and Juliet, if Romeo hadn't been such a poet.

She will work for him, stand behind him, and love him, even if she's giving far more than he is. She won't confront him—it's not her style. Eventually, she may use one of the "50 ways" to get herself free, even if she has to get on the bus. For a long time, she'll replay little scenes in her mind, trying to make sense of the whole experience. She realizes she did a lot of work for which he got the credit.

His confidence forces her to confirm her own beliefs. She realizes she can form an opinion *before* all the data is in, because it never is. And she knows if she doesn't ask for what she needs, no one will take the time to figure it out. At the least, she knows what she *doesn't* want in her next relationship.

with a Taurus:

When a Taurus guy puts his strong arm around her and gently squeezes her shoulder, a Pisces woman instinctively knows she has found a man who will protect her . . . and it feels like coming home. He has a quiet strength about him just as she does; she just doesn't recognize her own. As their relationship progresses, it just gets better. He isn't argumentative or critical. They seem to be of similar mind and purpose—to create a place that is a refuge from the world, one where peace resides and harmony reigns, at least most of the time.

Although she thrives in a stable relationship where she knows what to expect, she isn't set in her ways like him. She adapts to change; in fact, she *needs* change because she is always growing and changing herself. She won't be the same person tomorrow as she is today, and he must keep up with her personal growth or see them drift apart.

But even if he tries, he will never see the world the way she does. She wants to have a little magic, a little fantasy in her life, but he's a guy in love with reality. If it can't be seen, weighed, or measured, it doesn't exist for him. But she knows reality depends on who perceives it.

Still, they both appreciate the simple things in life, like a quiet evening at home and a delicious meal. And they can comfort each other when life gets too chaotic and noisy for him or too harsh and ugly for her.

with a Gemini:

Maybe she was having trouble finding a man when she took up with a Gemini. Why else would she get herself into a fix like that! The Pisces woman wants to believe everything her lover tells her . . . okay, she's gullible. With a Gemini man, though, *anyone* can be fooled. He can come up with an excuse quicker than Samantha could spiffy up the kitchen, so what chance does a trusting Pisces girl have to catch him in a lie?

It's not that all Gemini men are unfaithful, but he *does* have a split personality, you know, a Twin self, and just what that other twin has been up to is anyone's guess. Face it, he's not a likely candidate for True-Blue-Man-of-the-Year. Of course, it's always possible, but if he turns out to be a flirt, or worse, she can't live with it, or rather, she shouldn't. The stress can make her depressed, if not actually sick. What brought these two together?

For one, she's an interesting person, and he's fascinated by the insights she has about subjects he hasn't even thought about yet. He intrigues her as well, because he is so obviously intelligent and well informed. They have a lot to give each other. His chattiness will wear on her after a while, though, leaving her longing for a little solitude and quiet.

With a Gemini man, a Pisces woman will continue learning about herself. She will have the opportunity to see that her own needs are met, because he isn't going to do it, or even know what they are. He's intellectual, not emotional, so it's harder for him to be aware of her needs than it would be for a more *feeling* sign. It also doesn't come naturally to her to stick up for herself, but she has every reason to learn.

with a Cancer:

She needs periods of solitude to recharge her energies. As luck would have it, so does he! If they are both aware of this need in the other, they won't be hurt or misunderstand when one of them temporarily withdraws.

He understands human nature in a general sense, even if he isn't tuned in to his own deep feelings. She doesn't understand human nature on a mental level, but she is so tuned into people's vibes, it's scary. She can listen to the feeling behind his words and read his body language and facial expressions, so she understands his moods and gives him the space he needs.

Even though he can be gruff on the outside, he has a way of conveying to her how much he loves and appreciates her. He's not critical—except when he makes his sarcastic little jabs, but they are done with humor and, when he feels secure in *her* love, even directed at himself.

Once she has committed to him, she is almost too ready to give up her needs and give first place to his because it's her nature to selflessly serve another. She tries to encourage him when he's worried about work, but sometimes she picks up his despair and worries along with him. She doesn't expect things to be perfect, however, and she sacrifices a lot for the sake of their marriage.

He wants to handle the money and that's fine with her, but if they get in financial trouble, she realizes she should have taken a bigger interest in what was going on. He keeps many things to himself so she is blissfully unaware of looming problems.

with a Leo:

A Pisces woman can be happy in a variety of circumstances, as long as she feels loved and protected. A Leo man is emotionally prepared to do both. And she does the same for him because he brings out all the tender Pisces devotion she's capable of.

If he's a noble Lion, they can get along quite nicely. But if he's a lesser soul, he may begin to believe his own press about being "The King," and start to treat her like the servant who waits on him. A Leo man can be overbearing at times, and it's hard for her to stand up for herself. If she wanted to be assertive, she could learn to get better at it, but it's not her nature. She's more comfortable accepting limitations and just living with them.

He's happiest if he makes enough money so she can stay home with the children, but if she *does* work, he would like her to work from home, if possible. He won't admit it, but he doesn't want her to neglect him. This man takes more upkeep than any other sign. If she has a career that takes her away from home, or especially if she has to travel, he won't be as content or as giving; he may even become growly. As long as she has the love she needs, she can usually work around his ego and overlook the imperfect parts of their marriage. She tries to let him know, with her loving ways, that he is still the most important thing to her. Then again, she might discover once more, that love does *not* conquer all.

with a Virgo:

A Virgo man will never understand his Pisces mate, but what's new? Men have been saying that about women for a hundred years, or ever since they stopped thinking of them as property. In this case, it's true. He's a practical realist and she's a dreamer. He can never hope to do more than glimpse the mystery that she is.

For instance, he can't understand why she has compassion for every animal or person in trouble. It doesn't make sense to him and he sees it as impractical, even foolish.

A Pisces woman can be a procrastinator, which isn't good if he's the typical Virgo who wants a place for everything and everything in its place. If her mother-in-law is a perfectionist, too, she dreads her *white glove* visits. If he complains because she didn't pay the bills, she feels guilty and vows to do better. She doesn't mind if he gives her a nudge in the right direction, but sometimes he seems to enjoy pointing out her shortcomings.

On the plus side, she can lean on him. He can fix the garage door opener or build shelves in the laundry room. He's not the type to run around, and he takes his work very seriously. He likes his daily routine and, once she's adjusted to it, she likes it as well; it makes her feel more grounded.

One of their mutual interests is health. She knows that a balance between mind, body, and spirit is necessary, and she is well-acquainted with the holistic health movement. He relates more to traditional medical practice, but he's aware of the importance of diet and exercise. This can be an area where they encourage and educate each other.

with a Libra:

A Libra man is full of little surprises that delight the Pisces woman, like a rose, a bag of bagels, or tickets to a play, and he's so happy to have her there when he walks in the door, someone to talk to, eat with, and discuss business and family with. They both make the extra effort to be pleasant and supportive. There are differences between them, but nothing that can't be overcome with patient understanding.

Neither wants to spoil the peace and bring up something unpleasant. But even Adam and Eve had issues! Gripes that aren't expressed can lead to serious resentments over time.

There are two types of Pisces women: the quiet type and the talkative type. The quiet type processes information through her vast and deep intuitive, emotional nature; nothing is simple to her. By the time she decides on one of many possible responses, he has filled the long pause with words. The talkative Pisces just gabs away indiscriminately and doesn't give him a chance to reply. A Libra man enjoys exchanging ideas and likes the give-and-take of a conversation between equals.

Another difference is their comfort levels with the tidiness (or untidiness) of the house. Her mind doesn't dwell in a structured space. She can ignore clutter and disorder because confusion is something she is well-acquainted with. He is sensitive to a messy environment and likes everything neat and in its place.

She likes the occasional evening alone, but he never wants to go anyplace without her. She will accommodate him most of the time and claim a headache when she needs a little solitude.

with a Scorpio:

A Pisces woman instinctively knows that jealousy isn't a tactic to use with a Scorpio man. Her intuition comes in damn handy because he isn't going to divulge much of what's going on in his head. This is especially true if he feels strongly about something, and his jealousy definitely falls in that category. A Pisces woman can be seductive when she turns it on, which is what attracted him in the first place. But she's wise enough not to use it on another man just to get his attention.

A Scorpio man should come with an owner's manual.

1. Don't make him jealous.

2. Don't pry.

3. Don't make a joke at his expense.

4. Don't expect a Valentine's present.

It's a bit much to remember. Is this just another case of a Pisces woman attracted to a guy who's wrong for her? Perhaps not, if fidelity is a top priority—and when isn't it? Certainly all men can stray and statistics say that most do at some point, but a Scorpio man is into loyalty. He prizes it above almost anything, and although he's more concerned about loyalty on *her* part, at least it's in his repertoire.

She has an inner voice that tells her to "Make love, not war." But he has the passion of a vigilante and speaks of murder and mayhem, and that's just when someone cheats him or cuts him off in traffic. He scares her sometimes, but he never actually carries through, he's just venting his emotions. Perhaps she can heal some of his emotional wounds with her love and devotion—she certainly will try.

with a Sagittarius:

They're sitting around a campfire at night, gazing at the flames. She's poking at the embers with a stick and wondering, "Is he the right man for me?" He's thinking, "How can I get sex?" Ah, the differences between women and men!

A Pisces woman will find she has a lot of differences with a Sagittarius man. She is given to deep thought and contemplates the mysteries of life. He is daring and gregarious, with big plans for the future. She can imagine riding off with him into the sunset. They would both enjoy it, but she does it for the romance while he does it for the adventure.

She will need every ounce of her inner serenity if he's a lower type who makes promises he can't or won't keep. If he racks up credit card debt to finance his trips or his recreational equipment, she can get caught up in his lifestyle and trash her FICO score, as well as her dreams.

But many Sagittarian men are philosophical and, like her, ponder the big questions. If he's that type, he has a belief system he has worked out. A Pisces woman admires that in a man, and since she can see other viewpoints besides her own, they have many fascinating discussions. If he supports her search for herself, he can add a lot to her life. She needs someone to help her reach up, and a Sagittarian man can do just that. Ideally, trust is never broken between these two, because if it ever is, they will never be able to recapture the magic. Her dreams give her an escape from reality, while his dreams are objectives that he fully expects to attain.

with a Capricorn:

A Capricorn man is lying on a mat with his eyes closed, breathing deeply. Beside him is his Pisces wife, quietly instructing him to "visualize a beautiful place where you can relax." If his ego lets him, she can be a wonderful teacher who will help him learn breathing and relaxation techniques to release stress and reduce his blood pressure. This is one way she brings a new dimension to his down-to-earth existence. He brings security to hers.

He's a traditionalist who would just as soon have his wife at home caring for the family legacy, rather than pay someone else to do it. She will suppress her desire for a career if that's what he wants. The danger is that this lifestyle does not contribute to her as an individual and she becomes too dependent on him. Unless she has outside interests, depression can set in and she might escape to romance novels or, in worst cases, drugs or alcohol. In that case, he loses respect for her and perhaps strikes up a friendship with a woman who is more his equal. But like a child with her eyes shut, she thinks if she can't see it, it isn't there.

He balances out her leniency with the children with his brand of discipline so they get the best of both worlds. Sometimes she is unhappy when he works too much and doesn't give her the emotional support she needs. For instance, he has definite rules about spending, and if she doesn't live up to his expectations of financial responsibility, he gets exasperated and she feels inadequate. Even so, she still clings to the security he provides.

As old-fashioned as it sounds, a Pisces woman wants protection from the demands of life and the outside world. With a Capricorn man, she needn't worry; he's got her back.

with an Aquarius:

These two just might meet on the Internet. He spends a lot of time on his computer and she enjoys long distance affairs that aren't consummated—then her lover can remain on the pedestal where she put him and she doesn't have to deal with the harshness of reality.

But wherever they meet, she will be attracted to him because he's different from anyone else she's known. He's a complex guy, but a Pisces woman can figure out complicated personalities quicker than most. What she doesn't grasp intellectually, she tunes into with her intuition. If that's so, what's her excuse for getting involved with someone who lives a different life than she wants? Put it down to fate.

He likes to be in the flow of life and be out there doing things with his many friends and acquaintances. He might be a dedicated activist involved with an organization for social change or another group with a common interest. She likes people too, but she also needs time alone or to have an intimate dinner with a couple of good friends.

They can learn from each other if they're open to it. He's very rational in his thinking and looks at things logically. She uses her intuition and has her own way of knowing things that doesn't rely on proof or rationale. He can seem remote and cold to her when he doesn't show her the tenderness she needs.

A Pisces woman can put up with a lot of things that aren't perfect. A man with a personality that isn't exactly what she prefers is a small wave in the turbulent ocean of her life. If he provides stability and she can trust him, she puts up with the rest.

with another Pisces:

She knows how to clear the house of negative vibrations and uses Feng Shui to attract positive energy and allow it to flow freely through the rooms. He has his own beliefs, but he doesn't ridicule hers and, in fact, he helps her expand her insights.

If not actually artists, they are artist-types, and together they explore the poetic landscape and inspire each other. They both have an affinity for the ocean and love vacations by the water. At the least, they enjoy a big tank of tropical fish.

These two are gentle souls who are always for the underdog and can't turn down a plea for help. They sacrifice their own security for the larger good, like taking a lesser-paying job because it offers an opportunity to be of service. If they both work in the helping professions, they have another common bond. They would be a perfect pair to work behind the scenes somewhere.

They can both be confused by the enormity of life. They are attuned to mystical, artistic, or spiritual impulses instead of mundane concerns, so who will make the hard decisions? Ideally, they have a practical friend or relative from whom to seek advice.

Romantic love between two Fish is sweet, tender, and strong and grows deeper over time. Their high expectations won't be disappointed as long as he doesn't fail to convince her how much he needs her—and she doesn't withdraw when they have their rare arguments . . . and they hire someone to do their taxes.

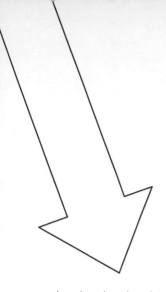

☆ ☆ ☆ ☆ ☆ ☆ ☆ ☆ ☆ ☆ ☆ ☆ ☆ ☆ ☆ ☆

PART THREE: ⊙n Your ⊙wn

How to be happy with him . . .
or without him. Look to your Sun sign
for your greatest strengths

☆ ☆ ☆ ☆ ☆ ☆ ☆ ☆ ☆ ☆ ☆ ☆ ☆ ☆ ☆ ☆

Prologue
What is your natural aptitude for living alone?

So you're alone. Maybe it's your choice and you're happy being single, at least for now. But even if you feel like roadkill on the highway of love, there's good news! You are actually face-to-face with a humongous opportunity! Being happily single is a skill and, like any skill, it takes a little practice. This is your chance to deal with the issue of being alone so you don't drag your fears with you into your new life, whatever shape it eventually takes.

Fear keeps many of us in awful relationships. We're afraid of having total responsibility for the bills, the kids, and everything that can possibly go wrong, especially the car breaking down. But besides the practical concerns, we're afraid of being alone.

A married woman can be just as lonely—even lonelier—with a remote or uncaring spouse as a woman on her own. If you've been there, you know that the wrong man is worse than no man at all. When you're actually alone, there are all kinds of things you can do to change your experience.

Solitude is part of our ordinary life and not to be feared. Admit it—haven't there been times when you would have given anything just to be able to finish a damn book in peace? It's when solitude is imposed on us that it's easy to slip into the "poor-me" habit of self-pity.

If you're on your own because your relationship fell apart, the real emotion is probably about being rejected or unloved or feeling like a failure, rather than the fear of being alone. In this case, you have the biggest challenge—to understand what happened and why—and to stop blaming yourself. A failed love affair doesn't mean *you* are a failure; it's just another episode in the work-in-progress that is you.

Your happiness is now in *your* hands and that's good: it means you can do something about it. Read how *your* sign handles breaking up without breaking down—and the traits you have that enable you to live a joyous, fulfilled life, whether there's a man around or not. If you know your Moon or Ascendant, look up those as well for more information.

THE SINGLE
ARIES WOMAN

You can fearlessly go where no man has gone before—because you're an Aries woman! Of all the signs, yours is the quickest to bounce back from a loss; nothing can keep you down for long. Your friends know you as upbeat and optimistic. When something isn't right in your life, you don't just put up with it. Your motto is, "When it's broke, fix it!" That puts you at the top of the heap (just where you like to be) when it comes to making a new plan for your life. False sentiment doesn't inhibit you, so you will thoroughly enjoy throwing or giving away everything that reminds you of him.

You might decide to move and start fresh in a place that is yours and yours alone, where even the couch you sat on together takes on a new personality. Even if you stay put, you can have things *your* way—no compromises: you have to admit there's a certain satisfaction in that. Before long, you'll begin to realize how much you enjoy being alone until solitude becomes a comfort. An Aries woman can handle the single life easier than any other sign.

One of your finest attributes is your independent spirit and the fact that you can make decisions. You no longer have to negotiate or pretend to need his input. You don't have to feel guilty for not telling him the whole truth about what you're up to; it takes so long to explain.

You have sometimes paid a price for being *too* pushy or *too* self-confident, in other words, *too* strong. Well, this is where it pays off. You aren't going to wilt now; in fact, you're going to blossom! Take a risk—do something you've fantasized about but never had the opportunity to try. If you're about to leap out of an airplane, climb a rock, or give a speech, you won't be thinking of him.

You kept your own interests and friendships alive, even though it sometimes caused stress in your relationship, and now you're glad you did! If you didn't, you were one of the rare Aries who let your partner dictate what you did or didn't do. All the more reason for you to see the bright side of this situation—there's no one to say you shouldn't do something!

The hardest thing for you is failing—you hate to lose at anything. But as soon as you realize it's your ego that's bruised more than your heart, you can begin to let go and move on. You have the power within you to stop suffering and change your outlook from a victim to a loving woman.

You are a romantic who believes in happily ever after, so even though it didn't work out this time, you'll never give up on the idea of love. In fact, the excitement of falling in love again will erase any lingering doubts and, eventually, you'll forget you ever said, "Never again" again!

Outstanding Aries women: Betty Ford, founder of the Betty Ford Clinic. Sandra Day O'Connor, retired Supreme Court Justice. Maya Angelou, poet and renaissance woman.

THE SINGLE
TAURUS WOMAN

Your friends wonder what took you so long! You knew for a long time your relationship was doomed, but you hung in there. It took a while to realize exactly what the problems were and still more time to try to fix them. But one day it happened, whatever "it" was, and you realized it was time to make the break. It all takes time and you can't be pushed. But now here it is—you're finally ready to start a new life. You know living in a nerve-wracking situation is the perfect formula for a stress-related illness, so congratulate yourself on making a needed change.

Your friends call you stubborn? Great! That's just what you need now. You can stick to your decision like no other sign. Once you've made up your mind, there's no going back. Unlike some of your friends who can resurrect a relationship, you are much too hurt. Something in you has died and you will NOT put yourself through it again. He could come crawling back with a red rose between his teeth and you wouldn't budge.

For a Taurus woman, little things mean a lot, like your beloved furniture, paintings, books, and sentimental trivia! You don't decorate to impress anyone; the things you have around you are the things you love. Of course your favorite chair or desk doesn't take the place of a man (or do they??) but be happy in your heart that you have them.

Now's the time to clean out closets, go through boxes, and throw away the photos, keepsakes, and gifts he gave you, unless you absolutely love them. It's hard to throw stuff away, but don't be saddled with things that don't represent who you are today.

As a Taurus woman, you're sensitive to your environment and now you can set the thermostat where *you're* comfortable. You derive a deep sense of contentment when cozying down in a comfy chair with a glass of wine or cup of tea and a good book, listening to your favorite music or watching TV without that constant channel changing that was so hard on your nervous system. You enjoy your own company and the peace that now prevails in your home. You get a quiet sense of satisfaction by having your little routines just the way you want them.

You might want to stay home too much, so get involved with a new interest now. Since getting started is the hardest part for you, ask a friend to join you in a class. Art, sculpting, ceramics, pottery, painting—all are good choices for Taurus, the most artistic sign in the Zodiac.

You have a strong body and like to use it, so working out brings you great satisfaction. Join a gym or walk regularly with friends to get in shape and lift your spirits. Be careful of over-indulging in food or drink, especially when you're down. Think about eating for health and quit the diets that lead to a vicious circle of deprivation and overeating.

To satisfy your skin hunger and enjoy the sense of touch we all need, make a habit of getting a massage. It gives you a feeling of well-being, it's cheaper than a doctor visit, and it's as good as sex . . . well, practically.

Outstanding Taurus women: Shirley MacLaine, actress, author. Katharine Hepburn, actress. Barbra Streisand, singer and activist.

THE SINGLE
GEMINI WOMAN

You aren't the type to withdraw after a break-up—you're way too friendly and outgoing for that! Chatting up the clerk at the grocery store or coffee shop, the drycleaner guy, or the bank teller keeps you from feeling isolated until you re-invent your social life. Just because it comes naturally to you, don't take it for granted, for it truly is a gift.

You're good at examining all possible sides of an issue and that's to your advantage. Even if you can't reason it all out logically, it helps you recover if you can determine what happened and why. Call your friends and tell them all the horrific details. They'll agree he's a jerk and tell you it's his loss and not yours—now *that's* therapy! Get it over with and then give it a rest. Your friends have a limit on how much they are willing to listen to you.

If you find your mind running rampant with a million worrisome thoughts, try focusing on what you see, hear, or feel in this very moment. It will stop your brain in its tracks. Since neither the past nor the future are here now, why dwell on them?

Contemplate that it isn't what happened that's hurting you, but your emotionally painful thoughts about it. As Deepak Chopra wrote in *Daughters of Joy*, "We line up our unsolvable problems like horses on a merry-go-round. Every day the same horses go around inside our heads."

Another strategy: Write your ex a letter listing all the ways he screwed up and how happy you are that it turned out as it did. Don't mail it, though. Keep it for the times you wish you were still together and re-read it then.

Curiosity is a basic ingredient of your personality, and variety is your spice of life. No one's better at learning a little about a lot of things, and now is your chance. Delve into those books you've wanted to read or subscribe to a new magazine—better yet, two magazines. You know you're a woman of many talents so take this time to discover what it is you want out of life. Look into some fun classes you might take. If you meet someone interesting there, you know you're starting off with a lot in common.

Alone in the evening? Jump on the Internet and indulge in all those Gemini things like connecting with others, gathering information, or just frittering away time in an enjoyable way. Play backgammon online or find a chat room where you can join discussions on one of your favorite subjects. Just don't try to meet your soul mate there!

You handle casual sexual encounters better than most signs, except maybe Aquarius. You might try that for a while as a diversion, but you won't be satisfied with that lifestyle forever. As women, we require more connection than that.

When you need a stress-reliever, jog or do some fast walking to get rid of anger and nervous tension. Take your mini iPod to the gym and listen to your favorite music on the stair-climber. Join a yoga, aerobics, or Pilates group—then you exercise and socialize in one outing—a double win!

Bottom line: A fresh start appeals to you—now's your chance!

Outstanding Gemini woman: Sally Ride, America's first woman astronaut.

The Single
Cancer Woman

The hardest thing for you to accept about being single is the issue of children. If you already have them, that's one thing you don't have to worry about. They'll see you through your biggest troubles and be a major source of love and companionship. But no matter how much you concentrate on them, you still need an adult support group of friends or family to help celebrate your happy events and commiserate about your sad ones. You don't have to feel alone.

The reason a woman recovers from a failed relationship quicker than a man is that she is so good at creating and sustaining emotional connections, and that goes double for a Cancer woman. You've always been a giver and you will find a way to keep giving, no matter what your relationship status.

If she doesn't have children, many a Cancer woman has found emotional nurture and unconditional love in her cat, dog, or other pet. It's a proven fact that pet-owners are healthier than those who aren't and that just stroking an animal lowers blood pressure and gets the endorphins flowing. That's one reason therapy animals can create miracles in hospitalized adults and children. Getting involved in an animal therapy group can be a wonderful antidote for your loneliness.

A Cancer woman's emotions run deep, so after you've been hurt, it's hard for you to love again. You may feel lost and hopeless for a while and won't want to put yourself out there; you just want to withdraw from the world. Be patient with yourself—you need some solitude and breathing room. In time, you will be ready to reach out and find new ways of relating, because it isn't your nature to be uninvolved with life or to be without goals.

Once labeled by astrology as homebodies, Cancer women are more likely than most signs to go for a new experience. When you're involved in something that challenges you, and you are accessible to growing and learning, your depression soon becomes a thing of the past.

You have a tendency to cling to people and things and your tenacious nature keeps you holding on to negative emotions. Anger can make you physically sick and your stomach could reflect your stress. Self-knowledge, perhaps through therapy, is vital so you can become aware of your insecurities, fears, and doubts. Astrology helps in self-understanding, so if you can find a professional astrologer you can relate to, go for a reading. Many forward-thinking psychologists are using astrology as a shortcut to get to a patient's issues.

You know there are no guarantees in life, except for change. People, even our beloved children, stay for a time and then leave. As long as you know the love that sustains you is within you and doesn't come from someone outside yourself, you can be secure in the knowledge that it can never be lost.

Outstanding Cancer women: Helen Keller—she overcame being blind, deaf, and mute to live an incredibly inspirational life. Actress Meryl Streep holds the record for the most Oscar nominations.

THE SINGLE
LEO WOMAN

No woman in the Zodiac has a bigger heart or requires more love than a Leo woman. Almost as important is your pride; you need to feel valued and respected, so when love fails, it's a one-two punch, right where it hurts the most! The pain is so great you have to stop and remind yourself that other women have lived through this and survived it and you can, too. You can play any role . . . from drama queen to survivor to giver. Now is the time to call on your acting ability until the way you feel inside matches the way people see you.

Don't be ashamed of your need for love, attention, and appreciation. It's not a sign of weakness; it's what keeps you striving throughout your life to improve yourself. One day you will look at yourself and realize you have become the loving, giving, accomplished woman you wanted to be.

The Cowardly Lion in the *Wizard of Oz* didn't know he was brave until he was tested. Maybe you're like that. But be assured—as a Leo woman, you have incredible courage. Somehow you will always muster the strength to do what is required and still maintain the love that is at your core. The early feminist and author Anaäs Nin said, "Life shrinks or expands in proportion to one's courage."

If you are without a romantic relationship, don't overlook the love and affection you get from the special people in your life, especially your children. There is one sure way you can live with love in your daily life—give it! If you don't have family, create family with close friends. Find someone who needs cheering up. When you do, you'll notice the sun beginning to shine again in your own heart.

Speaking of sun, a Leo woman needs sunshine and plenty of it. The Sun is your ruling planet, so get outside regularly and enjoy its rays. Best of all, take a nap in the sun.

Treat yourself as well as you would want a man to treat you. Pamper yourself with luxurious and expensive silk sheets and know that you deserve it. Put a facial, pedicure, and manicure on your credit card or take a bubble bath by candlelight. Find a massage college where students give affordable massages. Get a new hairstyle or change your makeup to go with the new you.

When you're alone, remember solitude is a gift. It enables you to tune in to what makes *you* happy, what touches your heart. It gives you precious time to pursue a hobby or interest. Check out a popular self-help book from the library; you're always looking for ways to become a more well-balanced and functional woman. Your natural optimism keeps you from getting too far down in the dumps, and giving up never crosses your mind.

Leo is the sign of creativity and you have an abundance of it. Discover the ways in which you most enjoy expressing it. Put your considerable talent and energy into what you love and watch yourself blossom.

One very important thing for you to do is get your body in the best shape possible. Besides the fact that you will banish the blues when you get your blood circulating and muscles toned, you'll be proud of yourself just for showing up at the gym.

Outstanding Leo women: Martha Stewart, businesswoman extraordinaire/TV personality. Amelia Earhart, the first woman to fly across the Atlantic Ocean and the first to fly solo across the Pacific.

The Single
Virgo Woman

You tend to keep your feelings to yourself, which makes it hard for your friends to know when, or how much, you're hurting. Let them help.

You always blame yourself first, so let up on the self-criticism—"What a fool I've been!" "Why do I always pick men with a fatal flaw?" "How could I have believed him?"—and give yourself credit for being the loving woman you are. A failed relationship is nothing to be ashamed of—even Nicole Kidman got dumped! Our self-esteem comes from within, not from a partner; why is it so hard for us to remember that?

Whether you're alone by choice or by chance, you are self-sufficient and can take care of yourself quite handily, thank you very much! If you can't do some of those household chores, pay someone to do them—and you don't even have to nag to get them done—what a relief!

You're on *your* timetable now! You can put in as many hours at work as you want without having to justify it; no more adapting to someone else's schedule or conflicting desires. Since you spend more time at work than at home, a co-worker/friend can be your support person, with whom you chat about matters both large and small.

Are you the typical Virgo woman who is up on all the latest information about healthful living? Then you probably already know that folic acid, B vitamins, complex carbohydrates, and omega 3 fatty acids can improve your mood. You're good at following new information about supplements, vitamins, etc.

If depression drags on, try therapy. Virgo, Taurus, and Capricorn women, more than other signs, believe in identifying problems and fixing them, so they are more apt to seek counseling. But maybe you're doing just fine. Studies show single women are happier than married women—but married men are happier than single men. Hmmm. Is there a message here?

You are particular about what you eat, so cooking only the food you enjoy is one of the benefits of living alone. You can eat what and when you want. Who said, "Freedom means I'm having Cheerios for dinner?"

Your friends may tell you to get a life when you spend days and weeks going through cupboards and closets, but it's therapy for you, not to mention fun. With each box of *his* stuff that goes to the Goodwill or in the dumpster, you'll feel lighter and freer. If he cooked, give away his favorite pans. Ditto the footstool he liked. Out go the memories along with the blue sweatshirt he left behind. The best part is that you throw out your anger along with the trash. Once you get rid of the things that most remind you of him, you can start replacing them. It doesn't have to be expensive. Get new throw rugs and curtains. Buy new salt and pepper shakers and pot holders. Get a new remote for the TV that doesn't have his fingerprints and body oil on it. Whew! That feels great!

Now is the time for a new start. You're good at crafts and like to be busy, so a hobby is perfect, especially when you're alone. Make a list of things you were once interested in and see if anything pops out. Flower drying? Miniatures? Tole painting? Find something you love to do and get involved.

Outstanding Virgo woman: Cathy Guisewite, who has won numerous awards for her comic strip character, "Cathy." The real Cathy married for the first time at age forty-seven.

THE SINGLE
LIBRA WOMAN

Now you can see the truth in the saying "What you resist, persists." The one thing you can't tolerate you now have to deal with—being alone. For a Libra woman, born under the partnership sign, it's not easy. You hate going places as a single; you're only truly comfortable with someone by your side—but like it or not, this is your chance to grow and develop your confidence.

If your ex was like most men, he relied on you to arrange your social schedule. Now that you're not together, you're in a better position than he is to maintain your lifestyle with friends and new acquaintances. But don't cram your day planner with things you don't really want to do and people you don't really want to spend time with to avoid being alone. On the other hand, you need people now more than ever, so if there's a movie or play you want to see, call a friend and go—don't sit home unless it makes you happy. If this all sounds like a delicate balancing act, well, Libra is just the sign that can manage to strike the right balance—eventually. In the meantime, remember that a woman in a marriage can be just as lonely as one living on her own.

An issue Libra women often have is stuffing their anger. They want to get along and they want people to like them, so they tend to give up their own desires to keep the peace. If you think you may not be in touch with your feelings, an assertiveness workshop or a conscious-ness-raising group can help. Any self-awareness you pick up now will help in all your relationships, present and future.

One of the most life-affirming things you can do if you're newly alone is to redecorate your place. Now you can choose the colors and styles that speak to you personally. With your talent and pizzazz, you can do wonders with drapes, pictures, and pillows, and not put much of a dent in the budget. You're sometimes *too* quick with your credit card, so don't fall into the shopping trap and spend beyond your means.

This is a great time to sort out your finances and make a plan, whether your main concern is paying off credit cards or opening an IRA for savings. Taking control and making decisions does wonders for your self-esteem.

Having something to look forward to when you're between boy-friends is important for a Libra gal. Check around for a games club—a group of fun-loving, social folks who meet regularly to play board games like Monopoly or cards, etc. You have so many connections with people it should be no problem to come up with enjoyable ways to spend your leisure time.

Outstanding Libra woman: Susan Sarandon, feminist and Oscar winner.

THE SINGLE
SCORPIO WOMAN

A Scorpio woman is the most self-sufficient woman in the Zodiac, matched in strength only by a Taurus, so you can survive anything. That's not to say it will be easy, but you can pick yourself up from any disaster and keep going.

You have many acquaintances but usually just a few trusted friends you can count on, women you know are loyal and with whom you have a history. Whatever the circumstance, you know they will be there for you emotionally, even if they are spread out across the country. Since you tend to keep your deepest feelings to yourself, confiding in your best friends gives them a chance to show you that they love and care for you.

In the case of a relationship breakup, the hardest part is letting go of the resentment or hate. Excellent advice was reiterated by Susan St. James when asked if she was angry about the death of her young son in an airplane crash. She said, "Having resentments is like taking poison and hoping the other guy dies." It's well-known what harboring deep feelings of anger and hate do to a woman's body, mind, and spirit.

You have a lot of power as a Scorpio woman, but you give up part of it when you see yourself as a victim. Remember that having a happy life is the best revenge. Now on to coping as a single woman.

You always throw yourself into a new lifestyle with your whole heart, and the single life is no exception. You want to experience it all in-depth: the freedom, the loneliness, the satisfaction, and the peace. You take things one at a time until you've mastered them all. Take a little thing like asking for a table for one, especially at a nice restaurant.

Dining alone can be intimidating if a woman is not accustomed to it. Like all fears, it is limiting and narrows your life. One Scorpio woman, alone after seventeen years, pretended she was a private eye following someone on a case. Sometimes she pretended she was a writer, investigating a location as background for a story. It was her little secret and it made a big difference in her comfort level when dining alone. Soon she was amused that she ever felt intimidated.

You love the time you have as a single person to delve into subjects you've had an interest in, but never had the opportunity to pursue. You are drawn to the unknown so you may further develop your psychic abilities or turn to meditation, witchcraft, astrology, or any number of esoteric subjects. You love reading mysteries and now you have the time to indulge yourself.

Once you're satisfied you've mastered the skills to be on your own, you begin to look around for your next challenge—an uncomplicated life isn't for you.

You know you can get whatever you go after, no problem. It's making the best choice that's the test, whether it's a man, a job, a house, or a lifestyle. There's something in you that wants to take on the biggest challenge. You take risks because you want to experience the heights and overcome the depths.

You may fall in love with being single; many Scorpio women have. You may develop a relationship with a man with no live-in strings attached. You may become very attached to your dog. You will always need someone or something to feel emotionally connected to.

Outstanding Scorpio women: Hillary Rodham Clinton. Julia Roberts.

THE SINGLE
SAGITTARIUS WOMAN

You can be happier single, especially if you were in a restrictive relationship with a man who didn't grow and change along with you. You require a lot of freedom because you have so many things you want to do in this life, so when you find yourself living alone, even after years of marriage, you adjust to it more easily than most. You can try recipes you know he'd hate and invite over all your friends that he disapproved of. as "flaky."

You may remain single much longer than your acquaintances. You aren't afraid of commitment. In fact, you're committed to many things: your family, your career, your pets, and your friends. But you love the freedom to pursue your dreams without having to justify them to a spouse.

Your positive attitude is your biggest asset. You always see the bright side of any situation—if today is a bummer, you're sure tomorrow will find you with a better job, more money, a nicer apartment, and an even brighter outlook.

One of your greatest pleasures is traveling, and when you're alone, you can plan the itinerary to suit yourself. Nothing is more exhilarating for you than taking off on an adventure. You can go alone and make friends along the way, or go with a group to a Club Med–style vacation or on a cruise. When you're single, you can be yourself and explore to your heart's content. If you meet someone interesting, fine, and if not, well, the point was fun and a new perspective. Plan one great vacation a year so you'll have something to look forward to.

If you're like most Sagittarians, you enjoy being outdoors and there's nothing like a beautiful sunset or exhilarating backpack trip to erase your worries and cares.

You can enroll in a college extension class or take an evening class at a nearby adult education facility. Your mind is eager to learn and being alone means you have the time to do it. Meeting people with compatible interests is a bonus.

Now that the buck stops with you, this is the time for you to get responsible about money. If you're in debt, contact your creditors and find out exactly how much you owe. Go to www.fico.com and get your credit report from at least one of the three credit bureaus and investigate anything that doesn't look right. Make a plan to raise your FICO score and try to save something, however small, for the future.

Maybe you never did go for the whole marriage thing—the wedding, the babies, the house in the suburbs. If not, there are many alternative lifestyles that can work for you, as long as freedom is an integral part of it. Who knows what lies ahead—something miraculous could be just around the corner.

Outstanding Sagittarius women: Bette Midler. Florence Griffith Joyner, Olympic sprint champion.

THE SINGLE
CAPRICORN WOMAN

One of the first things you want to do as a newly single Capricorn woman is figure out why your failed relationship ended so badly. You can't let it go until you thoroughly understand what happened. If you think it will help sort things out, you'll get counseling because you aren't the type to make the same mistake twice. Once you get everything organized mentally, you can enjoy being totally in charge of your life once more.

Every woman expects her marriage to last forever, but as a Capricorn woman, you had an even higher standard—perfection. Now that you know life—and your choices—aren't perfect, you can relax and move forward with a more realistic view. With time alone to think, you can determine what you want to accomplish and what direction you want your new life to take. You may realize you want to start going to church again or you might decide a different one is right for you.

It goes without saying you want to be a success at whatever you do and now you can really throw yourself into your work and focus your energies on your career. The more people you meet at parties and work-associated functions, the more you network and uncover opportunities. Who knows? You may find an even better job!

Women alone used to have to come to terms with a simpler life-style than they may have envisioned, but with your drive and ambition, there's no reason you can't provide well for yourself. Of course, you probably have children who will require much of your free time.

On the subject of children, yours are luckier than many whose parents divorce because you are capable of handing out discipline as well as being the loving nurturer. You set firm limits for them and they reward you by becoming well-behaved children and good citizens.

If depression is an issue for you, you will find a way to fix it, whether it takes working out regularly, going on long walks or jogs, or sitting by a full-spectrum light box every morning. Medication is a last resort, but you will do whatever is necessary if natural remedies are exhausted.

One area where single women sometimes don't do well is planning their finances, but as a Capricorn, you are better qualified than most to take on that responsibility. You probably didn't let your husband handle all the financial bits and pieces anyway, so it's not hard for you to take care of every aspect of your money now. You can sit down with your budget and figure a way to make it work. You will do without unnecessary things so you can squirrel away at least *some* money each month.

Since no one retains her youthfulness as well as a Capricorn woman, you can take your time to know yourself before getting involved with someone new. You may even have a fling with a younger man; in fact, it's not unusual for a Capricorn woman to take up with a man who is quite a bit older, or younger, than her. Now's your chance to let your hair down and be less serious.

Outstanding Capricorn women: Joan of Arc—as a teenager and heroine of France, she led the French Resistance against the English in the 100 Year's War. Clara Barton, founder of the American Red Cross.

THE SINGLE
PISCES WOMAN

You turn to your inner resources to get you through the most difficult times in your life knowing that, on a deep level, you are connected to something greater than yourself. Whatever form your personal spirituality takes, it's an important part of you and it helps you see the big picture when nothing else can. Going to a place of worship where you are with kindred souls will help you feel connected.

Don't punish yourself with feelings of inadequacy or thinking you should have known better. You can get caught in a negative mental state, reliving past conversations or betrayals. Let them go. Think about the miracle of this day, for it's all we ever really have.

You are so creative and intuitive that your life has endless possibilities. The symbol for Pisces is two fishes swimming in opposite directions, and that second fish is there to offer you a new beginning and a different perspective. Pain is inevitable in life, but suffering is optional. Everything depends on how you look at it. For instance, if you are involved in a relationship, some things are easier, but others are harder. Don't let yourself fall into the trap of seeing your life as a melodrama and yourself as a victim.

Use your powers of imagination and visualize the future you want for yourself. You know that if you can imagine it, it can happen. We all need time to reflect, uncover our own answers, and recognize our needs. Use this time to remember what you love to do and perhaps revisit the interests that once attracted you but were put on the back burner. Plan long-term goals to keep you on solid ground.

Use your creativity to think of ways to nurture yourself and encourage a sunny attitude. Music has a great effect on your mood, so invest in some new CDs. Indulge yourself with a painting that lifts your spirits and speaks to your heart. Keep a dream journal and explore what your dreams are telling you about your life. Smell has a powerful effect so try aromatherapy—using essential oils from flowers, leaves, etc. to influence your mood. Also try reflexology—it's a wonderful therapeutic tool for you.

When you are particularly vulnerable, as you are during a life-changing situation, your friends can be a source of strength, but reach out only to those who truly love you and want what's best for you. You are so open to other people's vibes—being around negative people brings you down, so seek out positive people.

As a survivor, you can come back stronger than ever. One way to feel competent and strong is to devise a plan for your financial security. Start paying off your credit cards, if at all possible. If your money situation looks hopeless, consider bankruptcy, but use it as a jump start for future responsibility. Give up your wish to be taken care of and know that you can take care of yourself. You will enter any new relationship with an inner security, more power, and less neediness.

Outstanding Pisces women: Drew Barrymore, actress and survivor. Queen Latifah, record and movie producer, rapper/singer, actress, talk show host.

Read unique articles by Llewellyn authors, recommendations by experts, and information on new releases. To receive a **free** copy of Llewellyn's consumer magazine, *New Worlds of Mind & Spirit,* simply call 1-877-NEW-WRLD or visit our website at www. llewellyn.com and click on *New Worlds.*

LLEWELLYN ORDERING INFORMATION

Order Online:
Visit our website at www.llewellyn.com, select your books, and order them on our secure server.

Order by Phone:
- Call toll-free within the U.S. at 1-877-NEW-WRLD (1-877-639-9753). Call toll-free within Canada at 1-866-NEW-WRLD (1-866-639-9753)
- We accept VISA, MasterCard, and American Express

Order by Mail:
Send the full price of your order (MN residents add 7% sales tax) in U.S. funds, plus postage & handling to:

> **Llewellyn Worldwide**
> **2143 Wooddale Drive, Dept. 0-7387-0954-9**
> **Woodbury, MN 55125-2989, U.S.A.**

Postage & Handling:
Standard (U.S., Mexico, & Canada). If your order is:
  $24.99 and under, add $3.00
  $25.00 and over, FREE STANDARD SHIPPING

AK, HI, PR: $15.00 for one book plus $1.00 for each additional book.

International Orders (airmail only):
  $16.00 for one book plus $3.00 for each additional book

Orders are processed within 2 business days.
Please allow for normal shipping time. Postage and handling rates subject to change.

Soul Mates & Hot Dates
How to Tell Who's Who

MARIA SHAW

Do you share a past life connection with someone special? Are you hoping to reconnect with your soul mate? In this down-to-earth, enlightening guide to karmic partnerships, Maria Shaw characterizes the many types of soul mate connections and offers advice on how to recognize your special someone.

Reuniting for love, paying a karmic debt, righting a wrong, or completing a higher purpose . . . there are many reasons why souls choose to meet again. True experiences of the author and her clients illustrate the dynamics of these powerful relationships that often involve our lovers, friends, and family. Maria Shaw also shares advice for achieving spiritual love, finding your soul's purpose, ending an abusive relationship, and seeking out the soul mate of your dreams.

0-7387-0746-5, 216 pp., 6 x 9   **$12.95**

To order, call 1-877-NEW-WRLD
Prices subject to change without notice

Astrology & Relationships
Techniques for Harmonious Personal Connections

DAVID POND

Take your relationships to a deeper level. There is a hunger for intimacy in the modern world. *Astrology & Relationships* is a guidebook on how to use astrology to improve all your relationships. This is not fortunetelling astrology, predicting which signs you will be most compatible with; instead, it uses astrology as a model to help you experience greater fulfillment and joy in relating to others. You can also look up your planets, and those of others, to discover specific relationship needs and talents.

What makes this book unique is that it goes beyond descriptive astrology to suggest methods and techniques for actualizing the stages of a relationship that each planet represents. Many of the exercises are designed to awaken individual skills and heighten self-understanding, leading you to first identify a particular quality within yourself, and then to relate to it in others.

0-7387-0046-0, 416 pp., 7½ x 9 ⅛   **$19.95**

To order, call 1-877-NEW-WRLD
Prices subject to change without notice

SignMates
Understanding the Games People Play

BERNIE ASHMAN

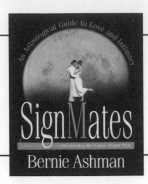

It is mystery and intrigue that leads many of us to play the relationship game, regardless of how our Sun signs are supposed to get along. *SignMates* dispels the myth that only certain Sun signs are compatible with each other. Any two signs can learn to establish a reliable stability. This book will show you how.

The "game" is defined as a repetitive pattern of negative behavior that interferes with the harmony of a partnership. It is an imbalance of energies, often of a subconscious nature. Take, for example, the "Missing the Boat" game played by Aries and Gemini. It begins when these two fast-paced signs continuously frustrate one another's actions and ideas. Aries' desire to follow immediate impulses clashes with the Gemini instinct to think before leaping. The challenge is to acknowledge one another's needs and potentials. By working through the strategies suggested for your sign combination, you can turn your differences into assets rather than liabilities. These pages will help you to better navigate your romantic encounters and create more effective ways to communicate.

1–56718–046–9, 504 pp., 7½ x 9⅛, 17 illus.   **$19.95**

To order, call 1-877-NEW-WRLD
Prices subject to change without notice